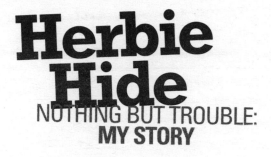

Herbie Hide

NOTHING BUT TROUBLE: MY STORY

Herbie Hide

NOTHING BUT TROUBLE:
MY STORY

HERBIE HIDE WITH GRAHAM MACLEAN

JOHN BLAKE

Published by John Blake Publishing Ltd,
3 Bramber Court, 2 Bramber Road,
London W14 9PB, England

www.johnblakepublishing.co.uk

First published in hardback in 2009

ISBN: 978-1-84454-706-7

British Library Cataloguing-in-Publication Data:

A catalogue record for this book is available from the British Library.

Design by www.envydesign.co.uk

Printed in the UK by CPI William Clowes Beccles NR34 7TL

1 3 5 7 9 10 8 6 4 2

Papers used by John Blake Publishing are natural, recyclable products
made from wood grown in sustainable forests. The manufacturing
processes conform to the environmental regulations of the country
of origin.

All pictures from the author's collection, except pp6-7, bottom p8, bottom
p9 © Marc Morris; p9 inset © John Hornewer; p8 bottom, p11 bottom,
p12 bottom, © PA Photos

For Alan, for ever my soul mate

Contents

Contents

Acknowledgements

As with any autobiography, this book couldn't have been written without the help of those people who have known me during my life, both privately and professionally. In the hope that I am not missing anybody, I want to say a big thank you to all of the following:

Helen, Henry, Haley and Hannah, just for being there for me and letting me do what I do.

My mum, Tina, and my dad, Alan Sr.

AJ Aban, Ian Allcock, Francis Ampofo, Richard Brearley, Bill Buck, Jackie Butler, Steve Butler, John Crofts, Graham Everett, Neil Featherby, Barry Hearn, John Hornewer, John Hutchens, Freddie King, Les King, Milton Lindsay, John Rollison and Rick Waghorn.

Foreword
by Barry Hearn

I first met Herbie when he walked into my gym in Romford as a stuttering, nervous and very shy 17-year-old. He told me he was a boxer and wanted me to manage him. I asked to see him in action and, as I had three heavyweights in the gym that day, he agreed to spar a few rounds with each of them. It was obvious that he possessed an enormous amount of natural ability; he had grace, movement and power, and handled himself with no problem at all against three very experienced heavyweights.

It is easy to say I was impressed – he had obviously styled himself on the great
Muhammad Ali – not just with his reactions and speed of movement, but with his power.

It took a few minutes to agree to look after him, and an incredible journey was
to begin.

Twenty-six fights later in a momentous evening at

Millwall Football Club, Herbie KOd Michael Bent in seven rounds to win the WBO world heavyweight title – job done!

He lost his title, but made a fortune, in his next fight against the awesome Riddick Bowe, but is still trading punches at the time of writing and, even at 37, looks destined to win another world title, but this time at cruiserweight.

Herbie possessed enormous natural ability but was never really big enough to emulate his hero Muhammad Ali. He was talented enough, but probably 2st (12.7kg) too light.

My time with Herbie was hugely exciting but Herbie could be difficult, as most top athletes can be. Having said that, I wouldn't change a day of my time with him – likeable, funny, but moody and demanding, sometimes he stretched the patience of a saint, but in that one great night on 19th March 1994 it was all worthwhile and, for that evening alone, Herbie will always have a special place in my sporting memories.

Barry Hearn
November 2008

Introduction

There is a famous football chant, sung on the terraces of The Den by the Millwall supporters, which goes, 'No one likes us, we don't care.' I know how those fans feel because, for as long as I have been a professional fighter, people have looked upon me as the bad boy of boxing – the pantomime villain whom the audience loves to hate. Even though I have enjoyed a more successful career than all but a handful of Britons, I have never experienced the support and adulation of a Lennox Lewis or a Frank Bruno. Many has been the time when the mere mention of my name has been greeted with a chorus of boos at a boxing match. Don't get me wrong: it's not something I get upset about. In fact, it has its advantages because, wherever I go and whatever I do, people will always be interested.

What do the public expect of me, Herbie Hide, the little African boy rescued from his Nigerian homeland who twice went on to win the heavyweight championship of the world? In their eyes I am the second baddest man on the planet, right behind Mike Tyson and marginally worse than Charles Manson. You only have to look at the newspapers and, more often than not, there will be an article about me. Usually it will tell of my latest scrape with the law, describing me with adjectives like 'deranged' or 'unhinged', while showing a picture of somebody or other walking away on crutches. It would be easy for me to sit here telling my story and claim that there was no truth to these stories, or that they were exaggerated tales of harmless little situations but, in fact, the reality is often more far fetched than the reporters would have you believe.

Success came quickly to me, bringing fame and fortune with it, but my life changed for ever with the death of my younger brother, Alan. In the shadow of this tragedy, my life spun out of control and I lost interest in boxing. The fights became fewer and my brushes with authority increased.

I live my life in a way that many people cannot understand, and while some have tried to fathom how I function, or what makes me tick, nobody is better equipped to offer an insight into my crazy existence than the person at the centre of it all. This is my story and while I tell it I want you to remember one thing: I am bad, but if I was as bad as people paint me then I would have been to prison and stayed there.

Chapter 1

Stranger in a Strange Land

It's quite normal to begin a book like this at the beginning. This is, after all, a story about my life and for most people that means from 'Day One'.

For me, though, my formative years began when I arrived in Norwich from Africa. I would like to explain a bit more about that first decade of my childhood, but the truth is that I do not remember very much about Nigeria. Of course, I know a few bits and pieces such as where I was born, and when, but much of that time is buried somewhere in a black hole at the back of my mind. Perhaps, subconsciously, moving away from my home had been such a traumatic experience for me at that tender age that I had no option but to block it out.

My father, at least the man I consider to be my father, brought me to England from Owerri, the city of my birth in the south of Nigeria, after he married my mother. Alan Hide adopted me as his own and lent me his name.

Nothing But Trouble

Young Herbert Okechukwu Maduagwu became Herbert Hide – Herbie for short.

I have read reports that my dad was a missionary in Nigeria, but this is not the case. He works in the petroleum industry and it was through his job that he first met my mum, Tina. He's originally from the Soho area of London, but settled in Norfolk as a young man before moving out to Port Harcourt. They married in 1982, the year that I moved to England, but they had been together for five years before that.

I was my mother's only child and, when she and my dad moved to England in 1980, I was left in the care of my grandmother for two years before they brought me over. There was never any contact with my natural father, so he couldn't have looked after me while they were away. We don't talk about him and I never needed him. I suspect he may be dead now, but I say that with some uncertainty. To me Alan always has been, and always will be, my dad.

At ten years of age I swapped Igboland for Norfolk. We moved into my parents' house in Lingwood, a village situated halfway between Norwich and Great Yarmouth, and it was quite a culture shock. There were so many things that were different from what I knew in Africa, not least the weather. It was summertime when I first arrived and by British standards it certainly wasn't cold. I remember gazing out onto our back garden from the living room of my new home. My parents were standing at the fence talking to Paul and Sue, our next-door neighbours, whose little boy, Andrew, was running around on the lawn with his fingers in his mouth and no clothes on. He would have been about three years old and I couldn't fathom how he could stand the cold. I had my sweater on and I wouldn't leave the living room, and even in there it was difficult for me to keep warm.

People have asked me if I encountered much racism in my new surroundings, but it was never really an issue for me. Perhaps I was too young to notice anything like that, but I never felt that anybody was prejudiced against me. I came from a mixed family, so maybe that made it easier for the locals to accept me. As far as I was concerned, my dad was white, my mum was black, and that was how my family was. It certainly helped me to be open minded and I never felt like an outsider.

Something many kids experience when they find themselves in a foreign environment is that the local children will pick on them. I was already big for my age, so the other children, certainly those who were as old as I was, didn't bother me in that way. It was easy for me to make new friends in Lingwood, as there were plenty of little rascals in the neighbourhood, and I went on to have some of the happiest days of my life in the village. There were plenty of us there, and even the bigger children took to me. But the boy I associated with the most was a lad called Paul Cooke, or Cookie for short. Along with the other children, we would go out picking peas and plums in the nearby fields, just having fun together.

Paul, the man who lived next door to us, had a cousin who would keep an eye on me. He would have been 16 or 17, an age I considered to be really old then and, together with his friend Jab, they made sure that no harm would come to me. I didn't know Jab at first but, when I heard that a group of older boys wanted to beat me up, it was Jab who sorted them out by warning them to leave me alone before letting me know I was safe. He was a really good kid.

I was heartbroken when my parents decided to move away from Lingwood. My mother was worrying about the way I was developing there. We weren't doing anything really bad, just hanging around the village in large groups as kids everywhere do when there is nothing to occupy them, and my mum imagined that I was getting up to no good. To the other children I was the main man and, whenever we got into mischief, I would usually be at the centre of it. My mum always used to worry about me then, just as she does today.

We eventually moved to Cringleford, a well-to-do village on the outskirts of Norwich, but it wasn't the same. I never made friends there in the same way and it was too far for me to visit my old mates in Lingwood.

Soon after my arrival in the country I was sent to my first boarding school, Glebe House School in Hunstanton. Even though my parents had the house in Lingwood, and later Cringleford, my dad's work dictated that he still needed to spend most of his time in Nigeria. Both of my parents wanted me to have the best education possible so they found me a place at Glebe House, where I could stay while they were away.

I was still unable to read or write and, even worse, I wasn't even proficient in English. I will explain a little more about my people in Nigeria, the Igbo people, later in the book, but you can probably guess that we would have spoken our own language in Africa and, while many people in Nigeria learn English, I had not yet reached that stage in my education when I moved to England. Most of the children in my year, local Norfolk kids, had been at the school since they were seven and I had a lot of catching up to do.

The school knew that my predicament was a delicate one and they acted accordingly by assigning another boy to take me under his wing and show me the ropes. His name was James Garner, although we called him Joel after the West Indian fast bowler, and at first I would try to hold his hand, something I quickly found out was frowned upon by the teachers at the school. Glebe House was an all-boys school at the time and, quite understandably, they didn't want to promote homosexuality among their pupils. In my case, though, I wasn't demonstrating any such tendencies. It is quite normal for children of any gender to hold each other's hand as a sign of friendship in Nigeria.

My experience after I joined the school was one of complete and utter isolation. Here I was in another country and far removed from everything that I had ever known. Aside from my communication problems I had never been subject to the regimental-style discipline common in an English boarding school. My frustration was overwhelming as I attempted to get to grips with this new academic way of life. The other boys would sometimes ridicule me and the only way I could respond, given my obvious difficulties with articulating myself, was by means of violence. Arguments would ensue and I would lash out at other pupils. This had clear repercussions and many was the time that I found myself standing at the notorious bell room wall waiting to see the headmaster, Mr Rolison. Back in his day, the punishment for misbehaviour was a slipper across the arse.

Perhaps I was fodder for cruel schoolboy wit but I have always hated having fun poked at me and I would always stand up for myself in such instances. There was an occasion towards the end of my time at the school when I had been involved in some sort of discussion in the playground. I think I had been beaten at a game and, poor loser that I was – and still am – I had burst into tears, much to the amusement of the other boys. A member of staff was looking on, a portly fellow called Mr Moss, who taught chemistry and biology, and he joined in with the laughter. This was becoming humiliating and to defend myself I said to nobody in particular – although the comment was clearly directed at Mr Moss – 'Some people are just so fat.'

Mr Moss went berserk, screaming at the top of his voice, 'You, get to the bell room wall – now!' It took me completely by surprise as he bundled me there by anything he could grab hold of. It was one of the few times in my life that I have ever felt afraid of anybody. He let me stand at the wall for a while but, even though I had insulted him, he never told the headmaster and I wasn't summoned for punishment. For me that was a sign of character and I had a great deal more respect for Mr Moss after this episode.

One of the best teachers at Glebe House, and also my housemaster, was Mr Brearley. He was a sports teacher from Pontefract in West Yorkshire, a particularly gifted rugby coach and geography teacher, who never believed in corporal punishment. Instead, he would try to coax the more troublesome boys. Mr Brearley commanded a great deal of respect among the pupils and most of us were more than a little intimidated by him. He didn't need to shout at people to let them know when he was annoyed and, for me, this was one of the most frightening aspects of his personality.

Although I was aggressive and quick tempered, I was never really bad. I just needed somebody to take an interest in me, to try to understand the difficulties I was facing and to show me that I was a valued member of the school. I was always a handful for any teacher and Mr Brearley was one of the few who really tried to understand me, and to help me.

In my boarding-school days I developed a sense of my own justice. If I believed I was in the right, I was quite prepared to take matters into my own hands, regardless of the consequences. If somebody was to make fun of me for not being able to read very well, or for having a pronounced stutter, they would get a smack. I was bigger than the other boys in my age group and people wouldn't usually make the mistake of upsetting me twice, but when it did happen I would react – and it was usually left to Mr Brearley to sit me down and explain the error of my ways, at least in my first year at the school.

Sadly for me, Mr Brearley left in the summer of 1984. The school was in transition after a change of headmasters. Mr Rolison had been left to handle the situation and Mr Brearley was one of the teachers who were holding the school together. Perhaps he would have stayed if the school had been able to offer him the security his teaching abilities warranted but, in the end, an offer from Gresham's School in Holt was too good for him to turn down.

His departure left a bit of a chasm for me at Glebe House. There were other teachers I got on well with, such as Mrs Hollingsworth, the English teacher, who taught me to read and write, but I was missing a strong male influence. Without that kind of guidance I became more unruly than I previously had been.

As with any school, there were a number of less-than-competent teachers at Glebe House. After my first year, certain members of staff were campaigning to have me expelled. It wasn't that I had committed any particular crime – I never lit any fires in the cloakrooms or brought drugs into the school – but I was becoming difficult to handle, getting into more and more fights with other boys. As far as I can gather they were uncomfortable with my demeanour. My size, coupled with my aggressive personality, frightened some of them. A good teacher should be able to guide a child and, if some of them were unable to do this, it says more about their suitability for their profession than it does about my suitability for the school. The school eventually asked me to leave and gave me a list of alternative schools where I might be able to continue my education. I went for interviews at all of these schools with my parents but, because my English was still not up to standard, none of them were willing to take me.

For a while it looked as if I would have to return to Nigeria. My mum and dad wanted me to be educated and, if that wasn't to be a possibility in England, they would have had no choice but to take me back to Africa. I do not believe that it would have come to this if Mr Brearley had still been at the school. Not only would he have known how to keep me in line, but I would go as far as to say that, given more time, he would have been able to temper the aggressive edge that brought me so much trouble later in life.

Stranger in a Strange Land

Thankfully, Mr Buck, the new headmaster after Mr Rolison's retirement, was able to see beyond the rugged, physical African. He appreciated my competitive spirit and my undoubted will to succeed, and he saw in me the potential to be a top-quality athlete. Unlike some of the teachers at the school, Mr Buck had no reason to be intimidated by me. He arrived at Glebe House from the Duke of York's Royal Military School in Dover, where he had at one time been the housemaster of the late Maurice Colclough – like me, a troublesome pupil – who had gone on to become a top-class rugby player and a member of the England team that won the Grand Slam in 1980. In any case, he was a strict disciplinarian. Whereas previously those lining up on the bell room wall could merely expect the slipper from Mr Rolison, Mr Buck would tan your hide.

The first time I saw him in action was when I had been misbehaving with some of my partners in crime at the school. We weren't particularly bad, but at age 12 or 13 we had outgrown some of the rules at the school. For example, we were expected to take a nap on Sunday afternoons after going to church while wearing a school cap. Then we were taken for regular walks along the beach, which would usually develop into fights among the sand dunes.

Towards the end of my time with the school they made me a prefect, meaning that I was allowed to leave the school premises at weekends. We didn't have much in the way of pocket money, so sometimes we would steal things from the nearby newsagent's. We were caught once after one of us tried to steal a packet of Walker's crisps. He already had them hidden in his coat but, because the crisps were making a lot of noise when he moved, he lost his bottle and decided to put them back. It was while he was doing this that the shop assistant caught us. I am sure that nothing would have happened if he had just walked out of the door.

It was after something like this that we finished up in Mr Buck's office. As he started to administer some well-placed whacks, I quickly switched places with a friend – not that it did me any good. Corporal punishment was part and parcel of life at boarding school in the 1980s and I don't hold a grudge against Mr Buck for using it. If anything, I would say that he was the person who filled the void left in my life after Mr Brearley left. In any case, I was never an angel and he had enough work to do disciplining me.

At that time the school had a reputation for producing high-quality sports teams. There was no football at Glebe House, so we played rugby union in the Michaelmas term, hockey in the Lent term and cricket in the summer. Rugby wasn't a sport I really knew much about in Africa and at first I had difficulty understanding the rules but, once I began playing, I enjoyed it. At first Mr Brearley would ask me to play as a back, despite my being bigger than the other boys. With my strength I could have been a good forward, but I was always very quick, so playing as a back suited me too.

Looking back, knowing how undisciplined I was at that age, I suspect that Mr Brearley wanted me to play in a position where I was unlikely to cause much trouble. Later on, after he left, I did play as a forward in the number-eight position where my natural strength was an asset to our team's scrum. Once I had the ball there was no stopping me. Because of my size and speed, there were very few boys who fancied tackling me and I became the leading try scorer for the Glebe House first 15.

Several years later, around the time of the 1995 Rugby World Cup, I bumped into an old classmate from the school and he told me that watching the huge Jonah Lomu wreak havoc for New Zealand reminded him of my performances on the rugby field. Lomu was a much more talented player than I ever was, but we did have something in common: people would see us coming and jump clear. Mr Buck will tell you that, if I had gone on to university afterwards (rugby union is that kind of sport), I could have gone on to play rugby at the very top level.

Some of my friends also went on to make a name for themselves as cricketers, among them Simon Bradshaw and James Garner playing at Minor-Counties level.

Glebe House also offered its boys the opportunity to try their hands at boxing and, for me, this was my first experience of the sport that would shape my life. A gentleman called George Gaines would come to the school twice a week in the evenings to teach the boys the basics of the sport. George was one of those people who are in boxing for the love of the sport. He was a local greengrocer with a military past who trained the pupils at Glebe House on a voluntary basis. There are a number of people who have helped me achieve what I have in the sport but George was the first to interest me in the magic of boxing and, if it hadn't been for his enthusiasm and dedication, I might have never even become a fighter.

When I first entered the makeshift ring at Glebe House it was an eye-opening experience. While I had always been quite handy with my fists, I knew as much about the sport of boxing as I had about rugby union. George asked me to spar with a boy called Freddy Case. Freddy had already done a bit of boxing at the school so he had an advantage over me and, before I knew what had happened, he had hit me on the nose.

The pain didn't really bother me much, although the thought of another person attacking me sent me into a rage. This lad had punched me and my first thought was to do something back to him. The rumour that went around the schoolyard was that I had reacted by kicking Freddy in the balls, but this isn't quite the case. I did lift my foot and certainly considered aiming a well-placed kick, but common sense got the better of me. Coming from my rough-and-tumble background in Nigeria, I knew how to fight, but I still had plenty to learn about the beautiful science.

Because I was so big and strong there were not many boys there who could hope to match me. We trained twice a week for 40 minutes through the Michaelmas and Lent terms and, at the end of the Lent term, there would be a competition between the houses. I wasn't able to take part because nobody was willing to face me, although in my first year they did ask Mr Brearley to take me on. I only heard about this later and it makes me laugh now to think that even he wouldn't fight me, because I was so afraid of him. After that they made me the honorary captain.

One year after I left Glebe House they put an end to boxing at the school. I'm told that it was the politically correct movement, more than anything else, that was putting pressure on schools all over the country to give up the sport. It's a pity because the kids who joined the school later would have had a lot of enjoyment from it but were forced to miss out.

Glebe House was a prep school, which taught boys only up to a certain age so, as the summer term before my 14th birthday ended, I left the school and joined Cawston College. In all honesty, speaking in terms of the characters you found there, the behaviour of the pupils and the standard of the teaching, it was a step down from Glebe House. It was much closer to Norwich, which was an advantage for me, but it wasn't really the kind of school that would support and nurture my athletic abilities, and it never had the kind of effect on me that Glebe House did. It also had a reputation for dealing with dyslexic pupils – something that didn't apply in my case.

When I joined I was the only boy in my year to be considered good enough for the first-15 rugby team. The rest of the lads would have been 16 or 17 but my size and skills helped me to get into the side, where I played in the number-eight position. They called me Bruno, after Frank Bruno (everybody in the school had a nickname), even though they didn't yet know that I was training to be a boxer. I was big, black and mean looking, so the nickname suited me. Once people heard about my training at Norwich Lads' Club they would call me by that name even more.

The school never managed to stimulate me. While I excelled as a sportsman, I had completely lost interest in the academic side of things. I spent every available opportunity at the Lads' Club when I wasn't at school and, in my mind, I was already destined to become a boxer. I knew that I could fight and that would be enough for me when I left the school.

Nothing But Trouble

There were two things in my life that mattered: boxing was one; my little baby brother was the other. I had always wanted a brother and when I was 15 little Alan came into the world. I was so thrilled at the thought of him that even boxing had to take a back seat for a while. He was one more reason for me to get away from this school and back to Norwich.

Otherwise, my attitude was terrible. When I turned up at my lessons I was only going through the motions. That says something about my dedication at the time, but also about the ability of the teachers who should have been trying to motivate me. There was one teacher at the college who was probably the most inept I ever came across – one of those people who cannot control a class. To be a good teacher you have to earn the respect of the kids and keep them interested, and he could do neither. We would sit there making fun of him. I used to sit at the back of his class in the corner of the room, beside a friend who was good at woodwork. One day he rigged up a mechanism to lower a toy spider from the ceiling onto the teacher's head. The spider was attached to a length of fishing line that had been threaded over some metal beams below the ceiling. This could then be controlled using a wooden pulley, which I was holding in my hand at the back of the room. Once the teacher had given us some work to do he sat down at the front of the class to mark some homework.

I waited until everybody had settled down and then lowered the spider very gently so that it was almost touching his head. I lifted it up and down, and after a while the other boys were all laughing. The teacher just looked at the class but didn't ask what was going on.

Stranger in a Strange Land

Again, I let the spider down a little and this time it brushed against his skin. Instead of looking up he just scratched his head. At this point the class was in hysterics. Then the teacher looked up and saw the spider. With his eyes he followed the fishing line all the way back to where I was sitting, now very sheepishly, in the corner. For a moment I thought he was going to hurt me because he brought out his pocket knife and walked over to my desk. I had never seen a teacher attack a pupil with a knife before, but there is a first time for everything. He swiped at the fishing line, cutting it so that the spider fell on the floor and I was left holding what was left of a useless pulley, and then returned to the front of the room without saying a word.

When I left Cawston College, after two wasted years and without any qualifications to my name, I was glad to see the back of the place. Finally I could get on with following my real purpose in life.

I'm still here but the school isn't. They had to close it in 1999. Boarding schools are expensive to run and they needed at least 120 pupils in order to keep the school afloat. By then they had 96 and, although several rescue bids were proposed, they were all rejected by the governors. Shame, I suppose!

Chapter 2

'I'm a B-b-b-boxer...'

Boxing was something I really enjoyed at Glebe House, but it was still something of a coincidence when, in the summer holidays after I left the school, I began training at the Norwich Lads' Club. I stumbled across the place while I was walking through the city. The club has changed its address a few times in recent years but when I first discovered the gym it was on King Street. What struck me initially was a poster on the wall outside, which showed a picture of a half-caste boy called Carmichael Kerr. There weren't many black people in Norwich at the time and Carmichael looked as though he must have been doing quite well for himself. For a few moments I stood gazing at the poster and then followed the steps from the pavement down to the gym in the basement.

Walking down those steps took a great deal of courage. I was 13 years old and still very shy because of my stammer, but that poster had struck a chord with me and

I wanted to see what the club had to offer. Boxing had always suited me at Glebe House, but that was against kids from a private school. Who was to say that they could even punch their way out of a paper bag? This gym was in the real world, where tough kids from poor backgrounds would channel their energies into something positive. These were guys who had never had it easy and who wouldn't take prisoners.

The gym was a horrible, dark, miserable-looking place with equipment that looked old. There was a stench of sweat as if old damp clothes had been thrown in the corner and forgotten about. This was boxing at its most primitive, the kind of scene that puts many people off the sport.

A man was standing close to the ring, so I approached him without introducing myself. 'I want to be like the boy on the poster,' I told him.

'You can't be like him,' he said. 'That boy has talent. He's a natural fighter. But you can be much better than you are now.' The man I was talking to was Chris Scott, a trainer at the club.

Norwich Lads' Club has a long and successful history. Since its formation in 1918 it has produced several top-quality amateur and professional boxers. The 1930s was a golden age for the club when its members included fighters such as Arthur 'Ginger' Sadd, who fought 250 times as a professional and once faced Jock McAvoy for the British middleweight title, and Chucky Robinson, who also went on to have a respectable career in the professionals as a lightweight.

More recently there has been Jonathan Thaxton, who went on to win the British lightweight title. These are just some of the men who went through the Lads' Club and had what it took to succeed in the paid ranks.

When I began training at the gym I obviously thought I was better than I actually was because I told Chris that I just wanted to spar.

'This is your first day,' he told me. 'We haven't taught you anything yet.'

'It's OK. I can handle it,' I said.

'Dickie,' he called over to Dickie Sadd, another one of the trainers there. 'Can you believe this guy? He says he's ready to spar.' They both had a good laugh at that.

This was all new to me and I had no idea that I needed to train before they would let me spar. Raw aggression alone wasn't enough and Chris made me learn the basics for a few weeks before he let me go anywhere near the ring. Even then, he chose to spar with me himself rather than let one of the other boys have a go. First he wanted to test my resolve by jabbing at me to see how I would react. I held my own in that session, but Chris was a huge, experienced man and he was able to handle me.

Once Chris was sure that I was good enough he let me spar with some of the older boys, and even with the professionals. Richard Bustin, who later boxed professionally as a super-middleweight, was seven years older than I was but I gave him hell in our sparring sessions. It was the same with Julian Bevis, a fine fighter who, I have to say, could have achieved so much more in the sport if he hadn't started boxing so late. He was a good test for a young boxer like me, but in the end I had no trouble dominating him during sparring.

Whenever my parents were away in Nigeria my dad would send over a monthly cheque to cover my living expenses, but the money didn't go far. I was always short of cash and, while 50p, the amount they charged at the Lads' Club, doesn't sound like a lot of money now, it was difficult for me to find back then. I wasn't the only one: there were other boys from poorer backgrounds at the club and they also found it hard to keep up. Nobody wanted to give up their boxing, so people would just forget to pay, or they would put it on the slate and hope that it would never catch up with them. It was just the same with me. That is, until I was brought to book about it.

The manager of the club, Ronnie Brookes, was well aware of the missing revenue so he asked his wife, Stephanie, to guard the entrance one day as the boys came in. She collared me on the pavement outside and said, 'Come here, you! You have to pay if you want to train.'

Thinking I was being really clever I told her to 'Fuck off!' and raced past her, down the steps into the gym.

Of course, she sent Ronnie after me. When he caught me he told me off for being so cheeky to his wife, but after that we had a long chat and I explained how I was trying to live on a shoestring. Ronnie could see that it was better to allow some of the boys, those who couldn't afford it, in for free. At least that way they would be in the gym doing something useful rather than out on the streets causing trouble. That was the first time I really had a dealing with him. Since then he's become a dear friend, sticking by me through thick and thin.

Stephanie forgave me pretty quickly, probably because she liked boys who were a bit cheeky, and after that we got along very well with each other. After my pro debut

I took my brother, Alan, to meet her. He was 15 years younger than me and had a confidence about him, even as a little kid, that Stephanie just loved. He would laugh and joke with her, and after that first meeting she wanted me to bring him with me every time I came.

All the boys at the Lads' Club had a crush on Stephanie. She would have been in her mid-30s and we all thought she was very sexy. We could never figure out how Ronnie, who would have been about 50, had managed to get her.

Once the summer holidays were over, I left Norwich for my new boarding school, Cawston College. Unlike Glebe House, Cawston didn't offer its pupils the opportunity to box. Chris had to convince them that boxing was a worthwhile pursuit, at least in my case, and that I should be allowed to visit the gym in the evenings. The teachers weren't keen but the headmaster, Mr Rix, was a fan of the sport. He believed that boxing taught discipline and that boys who were able to box wouldn't bother fighting outside the ring.

During those first few weeks Chris would drive over to the college and bring me back to the gym so that I could continue to train on a regular basis. He was sure that I had what it took to be a successful boxer, maybe even a champion one day. I would arrive at the gym still wearing my school uniform and then spar with whoever was there. One or two of the other lads claimed that I was older than I said I was, but I put that down to envy. I was just the best boxer ever to come out of Norwich and for some of them it was hard to accept that I had so much ability at such a tender age.

There are a lot of boys who box during the holidays

and then forget all about it when they go back to school. The same probably would have happened to me if it hadn't been for Chris's belief in me.

Chris continued to collect me for the first couple of months but then suddenly he stopped coming. It left me completely shattered, as if somebody had died. All that mattered to me was my boxing and without Chris to pick me up there was no way that I could continue training during term time. My schoolwork suffered because I couldn't concentrate on anything. It was sad but after that my time at the gym was limited to the school holidays.

The school contacted Chris after they saw the change in my attitude. They told me that his wife had put a stop to it, that she had told him that it was a waste of time to drive all the way to Cawston and that I was going nowhere as a fighter. I am not sure how much she thought she knew about boxing, but it must have had an effect on Chris.

Once I left the college it was a huge relief because it meant that I could dedicate all my time to the gym. While I was at school I couldn't train properly, at least not over a long period of time, and I think this is the main reason why I didn't have a long amateur career. In my mind, I was certainly good enough to have been fighting on amateur shows but I needed the kind of continuity in the gym that wasn't possible while I was at boarding school. It was only after I left that I could buckle down and start working towards some proper fights.

I couldn't wait to get started. After so many years of training and preparation I was finally going to be able to get in the ring with somebody and knock them spark out.

'I'm a B-b-b-boxer...'

It was such a good feeling to call myself a fighter at last. Everybody in the gym knew that I had the potential to do well in boxing, but that potential counts for nothing if you don't get the opportunity to prove it.

Too much time had already been wasted. Those years trapped inside the walls of Cawston College had meant that I had never had the chance to fight as a junior so, when I did finally climb through the ropes, it was as a senior. I enjoyed a short, explosive spell as an amateur, which lasted about a year and, even though I lost one of my earliest fights, I was still too much for most lads to handle. That's why, before long, the Lads' Club decided to enter me for the Amateur Boxing Association (ABA) national championships.

At the beginning of that 12-month period a friend of mine at the gym called Sean King told me that his father, Les, was interested in providing some financial backing. I was 17 and I had just had my first amateur fight when he agreed to sponsor me. Les, who ran the Regal Cinema in Norwich when I first met him, is very well known in Norfolk. He's a former boxer and local businessman who passionately follows all kinds of sports in the area. I could not help liking Les, a true gentleman who offered me friendship and encouragement throughout my time in the amateurs and well into the early days of my professional career. Many was the time he would pick me up in his car and take me for something to eat, and not once did he let me pay for the meal. Even after I had become successful and had millions in the bank, he still wouldn't let me put my hand in my pocket.

A jack of all trades, Les then took to writing and brought out three books, *King of Sport* (1, 2 and 3), about his sporting experiences in Norfolk. Needless to say, he had a fair bit to say about me in those. Les used to make me laugh. He was obsessed with boxing and even fought several times himself, mostly as an amateur, but he did compete as a professional once or twice.

Sean was useful enough, but I always thought that he was doing it for the sake of his dad. Les was a judge for the Lads' Club. I think Les would have been delighted if Sean had fought as a professional but, after Sean's mate Mark Goult was badly injured against Danny Potter in a fight at Norwich Sports Village in 1990, he decided to call time on his own boxing career.

Injuries like that are part and parcel of the sport. I once saw Margaret Thatcher say on television, after an MP had been murdered, 'We always think it will only happen to somebody else.' That sums up my attitude as a boxer. I know that the sport has its risks and I have known people who have been hurt in the ring, but I have honestly never believed that something like that could happen to me. I imagine that many boxers feel the same – if we didn't, we would be too afraid to fight.

As far as I was concerned, I had an excellent chance of being successful as an amateur. I was supremely confident and, under the watchful eyes of club trainers John Hutchens and Martin Flaherty, I expected to win easily every time I fought. Not everybody felt the same though. We had a rival boxing club in Norwich called the Broadside ABC. A guy called Ray Pease ran the place. While I was competing in the ABA championships, he said to me, 'Never mind winning the tournament, you'll do well if you can get past the Eastern Counties.'

Clearly he didn't share the belief that some of the trainers at the Lads' Club had in me, so I told him that I thought I would do much better than that.

'Those London boys are the ones you have to watch out for,' he warned me.

I wondered what he was talking about. There was no need for me to be afraid of anybody, whether they came from London or anywhere else on the planet. I was Nigerian and we believed that the European boys were all weaker than we were. Fighting was in our blood. Even so, Ray's words had been a major blow to my confidence. Boxing is a mental sport as well as physical, and a fighter thrives on encouragement. I had to dig very deep in order to pull myself through this crisis.

When I fought Martin Brown at the Lads' Club in the Zone finals, I boxed beautifully to outpoint him clearly, and Ray Pease was there to watch me. The place was full and everybody was singing my name. I think that showed Ray just how good I was. He shook my hand after that and said, 'Well done, son.' I had made him swallow his words and now he knew that he had misjudged me.

It wasn't just Ray who had been impressed though. There was an announcement over the Tannoy system to say, 'Herbie Hide has done Norwich proud.' I was now the Eastern Counties ABA heavyweight champion for 1989.

Actually, the regional coach had asked John Hutchens to withdraw me before the fight. He felt that I was too inexperienced to be fighting at this level and that there was a chance that I would be badly hurt. John refused, knowing very well that if anything did happen to me he would lose his licence as a trainer. He had complete faith in me and I repaid him in style.

Something else John would do was to tell me that my opponents were even more inexperienced than I was. This was to settle me before a fight, and I would go in there believing I had nothing to fear. It was only later, after I had read the newspaper reports, that I would realise I had been fighting a 30-year-old veteran who had 300 amateur bouts behind him.

We travelled over to Gloucester for the semi-finals of the ABAs and there I fought Denzil Browne, the North East Counties ABA champion. I stopped him in the third round, which meant that I would progress to the final. It was a good result for me considering that Denzil was rated as the third-best heavyweight in Britain at the time.

At an event like that you meet fighters from all over the country, rather than just the Eastern Counties boys. I hadn't really met any of these boxers before, but there was one guy in particular who stood out. He was a funny looking little man from Ghana called Francis Ampofo, who was actually more than four years older than I was, but he looked so small, as if he should have had a dummy in his mouth. I approached his table while he was eating a meal and asked, 'Are you a boxer?'

'Yes,' he replied.

'How old are you?'

'I'm twenty-two.'

'Have you got a girlfriend then?'

'Yes.'

I couldn't believe it. How could this little guy have a girlfriend when I didn't? Away from the gym I was still very shy and naïve. So far I hadn't been able to meet a girl and I felt a bit insecure about it. When I heard that this little guy was more successful than I was with the ladies, it made me feel even worse. Life wasn't fair.

I fought Henry Akinwande in the final of the ABA National Championships. The fight took place at the Wembley Arena on 3 May 1989 and it was always going to be a difficult task. Henry, who was the London ABA champion, was also the defending champion after winning the tournament the previous year. I needed all the support I could get, so Les King organised a bus from Norwich so that all my friends from the Lads' Club could cheer me on.

This was also the first time that my parents found out I had been boxing. My mum, who has always been very protective of me, wouldn't have approved when I first started visiting the club, so I told her that I had been playing football. It had been a handy excuse then and I'd never got around to telling her what I was really up to. It was my Auntie Winnie who put her in the picture. She knew everybody in Norwich and, once I started to become a minor sporting celebrity in the city, it didn't take long for her to hear about it.

Losing on points was disappointing but, at the same time, it was only my tenth fight. Henry was six years older than I was and he had a great deal more experience. He had been selected for England a few times, so that tells you something about his pedigree. Most people thought I held my own against him and, in the end, it was pretty close on the scorecards, but he was just a bit too good for me. Even then, with his long arms and awkward style, he was difficult for anybody to face, just as he would be later as a professional.

Nothing But Trouble

If I had won that fight then, at 17 and with only 10 amateur fights, I would have been the youngest and most inexperienced ABA heavyweight champion ever. Frank Bruno, who was 18 when he won the title and had fought 20 times, held the record.

Amateur boxing had always been a means to an end for me. What I really wanted was to become a professional fighter, and this dream started to become a reality when we met Freddie King through Chris Elliot from the Lads' Club. They had a chat about me, and Freddie, who worked as a trainer at the Matchroom gym in Romford, suggested that I should come along so that Barry Hearn, the sports promoter and owner of Matchroom, could take a look at me.

Chris went along with me to Romford. He was an experienced former boxer himself and fought against Freddie King in the early 1960s, although by the time I first met him he had been confined to a wheelchair through multiple sclerosis. I was also friendly with his son Carl, another young boxer from the Lads' Club.

Barry Hearn will tell you that when he first met me my arse was hanging out of my trousers. He can say what he wants – I went to a better school than he did. It's true, though, that I sent a mixed message to him when we first met.

When he saw me for the first time he asked who I was. 'I'm a b-b-b-boxer,' I told him.

'If that's the case, let's have a look at you.' He obviously wasn't convinced yet, but that would soon change. He let me spar with a seasoned professional called Jess Harding and I battered him all over the ring. There was another lad there that day, Phil

'I'm a B-b-b-boxer...'

Soundy, who was about to turn professional, and he lasted only a round with me. That certainly grabbed Barry's attention.

Chapter 3

Matchroom

The big news as I celebrated my 18th birthday – with a barbecue organised by my parents for all my friends from the Lads' Club – was that Barry Hearn had offered me terms to turn professional with his stable of boxers in Romford. It meant that I would be training in Essex during the week and then coming back home to Norwich at the weekends. It also meant that I would be mixing with top boxers on a daily basis, something that could only benefit me as I made the transition from amateur to professional.

There were some classy professionals who were fighting for Matchroom at the time. Mark Reefer, who held the Commonwealth lightweight title, was one. Then there were Jimmy McDonnel, Chris Eubank and Carl Crook. Actually, I never got on very well with Carl because he would make fun of my stammer. It was just a childish thing and today I would know better than to worry about it, but at that stage it got under my skin.

Nothing But Trouble

I was delighted to be taken on by Barry because he had a reputation for being one of the best promoters in the business. Barry qualified as a chartered accountant after leaving school, but it was for his activities in the world of snooker that he became famous. In the 1980s, when snooker was still popular, he had many of the best players under contract at Matchroom. Top stars such as Steve Davis, Jimmy White and Dennis Taylor were all signed to Barry.

It wasn't until 1987 that he promoted his first boxing event when he staged Frank Bruno's fight against Joe Bugner at White Hart Lane in front of 30,000 fans. After that he built up a successful stable of boxers and promoted some of the most important fights to take place in Britain in the last 20 years.

Matchroom also had the financial clout to provide me with quality training and sparring. The gym there was better than anything I had ever seen before, although at first I found it difficult to adjust to the regime there. I was placed under Darkie Smith's tutorship and I didn't feel that we really clicked. As an amateur I had been lucky enough to train under John Hutchens, who had helped me to turn my speed into a major asset. The training under Darkie didn't really seem tailored to my strengths.

At first I stayed in a hotel. Freddie King showed me to my room and told me when I was to get up in the morning, and that I should run for half an hour before reporting to training.

'Who am I supposed to run with?' I asked him.

'There's another lad across the corridor,' he replied. 'We can ask him if he'll run with you.' We knocked at the door and Chris Eubank opened it. Freddie asked him if he wanted to run with me.

'I don't run with anybody else,' he said. 'I run by myself.' I was young and away from home. I was so happy that there was somebody close by whom I could associate with in the hotel, and then he went and said that. These days he is well known for being arrogant and eccentric, but this was before he had become famous and I just thought that he was a complete arsehole.

The next time I saw Chris was in the gym, and I was asked to spar with him. This was fine by me. After he had been so rude in the hotel I took great delight in smashing him all over the ring. He was much more experienced than I was, but he couldn't cope with my jab.

Then a funny thing happened. He saw me skipping at the gym and started skipping next to me. Perhaps he liked to run alone but he certainly had no reservations about skipping with me. I just thought that he was a bit weird.

'Where did you learn to box?' he asked me.

'Norwich,' I told him. I wasn't sure what he wanted from me but it was clear that the hiding I dished out to him in the sparring session had instilled some respect into him.

'Where's that then?' he asked.

It turned out that he wanted to get me back into the ring. I had embarrassed him in that first training session and he hoped to prove to himself that he was far too good to be troubled by a novice like me. None of that mattered to me because, as far as I was concerned, I would spar with anybody and I was quite happy to have a second session with Chris. He tried much harder this time but, again, I got the better of him. I was too quick for him and he could hardly hit me. All the while I was beating him back with my jab. Darkie Smith was shocked at how well I handled Chris.

Chris came back to me afterwards and asked, 'How was that body shot?'

'Which body shot?' He had actually got through to my midriff with a couple of decent punches, but not enough to trouble me. Actually, the only punch he had really attempted to hit me with was a straight right to the body. More than anything else, it was psychological for him. He wanted me to admit that his punches had hurt me so that he could reassure himself it had not just been one-way traffic.

'Chris,' I said. 'Get the fuck out of my face!' I didn't want to play his games and after that we didn't speak for a long time, not until shortly before my first fight.

It was only later that I heard it was Barry who had asked Chris to spar with me. 'I have this young kid,' he told him. 'Can you spar with him?'

'Barry, no. I'm a pro and I don't want to be sparring with kids,' was Chris's reply. Barry can be persuasive though, and eventually Chris relented.

When Barry asked how the session had gone, Chris told him, 'You have an unpolished diamond. Please don't ask me to do you any more favours like that.'

A couple of months after my 18th birthday I stepped into the ring for the first time as a professional. I was fighting on the undercard of a bill featuring, among others, Errol Christie and Chris Eubank at the York Hall in Bethnal Green. My opponent was Lee Williams, an inexperienced boxer who had drawn one and lost one of his two previous fights. I knocked him out in the second round.

It felt very easy going into that fight. In the amateurs I had been fighting at a high level, culminating in the fight with Henry Akinwande, so this was like starting again at a lower level. It was the kind of fight to set a promising youngster on his way. Williams was never going to give me a competitive fight, but getting the first win on my record was very important to me, as it is to any young professional. The Dancing Destroyer, named after the Apollo Creed character in the *Rocky* films, had arrived!

I travelled back to Essex with Barry in his limo, driven by his chauffer, Robbo. Barry was good with his fighters in that way. He had class and always looked after me in style. We sat in the back of the car watching the fight on video and I felt on top of the world.

Looking back, I think Barry took to me because I was such a naïve kid. I remember that he once took me to an expensive clothing outlet in Ilford, where he fitted me out with designer suits. We went there in his Mercedes but afterwards he had an appointment in London, so he gave me the keys to the car and told me to make my own way back. I was so nervous because I had never driven a car like this before. Once I had decided that it would probably be a bad idea to steal it, I just thought to myself, 'What a life this guy has.'

My second fight, against Gary McCrory, followed 12 days later, again in London but this time in the Royal Albert Hall on the undercard of Jimmy McDonnell's title challenge against Azumah Nelson. It finished in disappointment for Jimmy after he was stopped in the

12th round, but for me it was a good night. I stopped McCrory in the first round.

I had one more fight before Christmas, back at the York Hall, where Steve Osbourne took me all the way to the sixth and last round before I eventually stopped him. I injured my hand in that one and was ruled out for a few months while I waited for surgery.

During that lay-off my trainer, Darkie Smith, left the Matchroom stable and Freddie King took over. For me it was a blessing because I began to prosper under Freddie. Darkie had taught me how deliver a straight right to the body after landing a left jab to the head, showing me how to use those two punches to keep pushing the opponent back. With Freddie I was able to learn much more about combination punching.

Freddie has an incredible boxing mind. There are certain people who can read boxing matches like musicians can read notes, and Freddie is one of them. He would know how the other boxer was going to fight, what his boxer needed to do to counter the other boxer, and how the fight would finish. As a former fighter himself, Freddie had studied the game to become a great trainer. Among others, he watched Sugar Ray Robinson when he fought in England and wrote down the combinations he used so that he could instil them into his own brand of coaching.

What he taught me about combination punching was that there's no point in attempting a complicated series of punches, which is never likely to work. His combinations were simple but effective. He showed me how to jab, fire a right to the body, a left hook to the head and then finish with a right hand to the head. It was easy to follow and, because of my hand speed, it could spell trouble for my opponents. The combinations became instinctive. I would go into the ring and, without thinking about what I was doing, I could just deliver them perfectly. That's why so many of my fights ended early – the guys I was fighting, who were not top-class boxers anyway, had no answer for this machine-gun kind of attack.

Later in my career, since parting with Freddie, I have relied more on a double jab followed by a straight right. I have had some good trainers but only Freddie was able to hold the pads correctly for those kinds of combinations, and once you stop practising you lose the ability to deliver them.

During that first year, I stayed at a house in Brentwood throughout the week. Four of us shared the place: Errol McDonald, Tony McKenzie, Ian Allcock and I. I would have been 18 years old when I moved in and my housemates, who were all 7 or 8 years older than I was, looked upon me as the baby of the house.

The house wasn't far from Romford, so it was handy for us. Each of us was involved in boxing, with Ian being employed as a trainer at Matchroom while Errol and Tony were fighters there. Not everybody understands how a boxer functions and how he needs to live, so it was beneficial for me to be around people who understood the sport.

The problem was that, when we weren't training, we would often become bored, sitting around in the living room, just watching television because there was nothing else for us to do. It was at times like this that banter would start, often with me as the butt of the joke. I had spent several years in boarding schools while the other three were men of the world, so it's not surprising that they found me naïve, just like the time I decided that we needed a pet to keep us company. As normal, we were watching the box when I turned to the others and said, 'I've got an idea. Let's get a parrot and teach it to talk.'

The others just looked at me, thinking that I was being daft. Then Ian replied, 'That would be good, Herbie. You can sit there and teach it. We'll have the world's first stammering parrot.'

They saw me as a bit of a clown, and I probably was at that age – even if I didn't mean to be. And it wasn't just the way I talked. There was a time when I had dreadlocks attached to my hair, thinking that it would make me look cool. However, nobody ever saw me in public with them for a couple of reasons. The first was that Barry thought I looked like a prat and told me to get rid of them. The second was that they weren't very well fixed and they started to fall out all over the house. Errol collected them all from the carpet and tied them together to make a skipping rope for me.

Then there was the time I had my first car, a Volvo, which I thought had broken down one night just as I was approaching the house. I left it in the middle of the road. The next morning I woke to the sound of people shouting and sounding their horns as milk floats and delivery vans had to try to manoeuvre around it. I never thought that the neighbours would realise it was mine, but they did – probably because it had HERBIE HIDE – FUTURE CRUISERWEIGHT CHAMPION OF THE WORLD plastered on its paintwork, complete with a picture of a red boxing glove. As it turned out there was nothing wrong with the car – nothing that a tank of petrol wouldn't fix.

I was still a novice at Matchroom and being around more experienced men helped me to grow up and understand the other fighters. Boxers might seem to be tough on the outside but often they have a very fragile psyche. There was a middleweight at the gym called Errol Christie who could have been an outstanding boxer. In the gym he would smash Chris Eubank around the ring in sparring, but when he fought for real he just wasn't the same. He'd win some, he'd lose some, but he never achieved what he could have done considering the talent he possessed.

In November 1990 he was matched with Michael Watson in Birmingham on the undercard of the first fight between Eubank and Nigel Benn. It had been a good night for most of the Matchroom boys, starting with me, beating Steve Lewsam and stopping him in the first round of my eighth professional outing, and Errol McDonald also recording a victory before Chris stopped Nigel in the brutal main event. For Errol Christie it was a disaster. He was stopped in the third round and afterwards he began to question whether he had a future in the sport.

People at Matchroom were talking about Errol, saying that he was finished as a fighter, but they wouldn't tell him to his face. When he dropped into the gym to pick up his cheque for the Watson fight, he joined up with a few of us in a local café for a bite to eat. Jimmy McDonnel was there, as were Ian and Errol McDonald. Errol Christie was down in the dumps and asked us what we thought he should do. We all sat there quietly, with nobody prepared to repeat what they were thinking out loud. I had been listening to Darkie Smith all day, telling everybody that Errol should quit, so I decided to break the ice. 'Errol, Darkie says that you should—' Just as I was starting to stammer Ian kicked me from under the table. It wasn't what Errol needed to hear at this moment. I had never taken a beating before and was too immature to understand what Errol must have been going through. Ian stopped me just in time and I changed the end of my sentence to, '. . . carry on boxing.'

My first few fights took place in the cruiserweight division, but when I met David Jules at the Grosvenor House Hotel in Mayfair in April 1991 I was fighting as a heavyweight for the first time in my ninth professional bout. It didn't worry me at all. I was quick enough and I punched hard enough to beat almost anybody I was matched with, and this I proved by stopping Jules in the first round. It just goes to show that if I'm faster than you are, you're in trouble!

Freddie's philosophy was that I should grow into the heavyweight division naturally. When I began I weighed in the region of 13-and-a-half stone. Freddie thought that there was no point in matching me with guys weighing 16-and-a-half stone until I was big enough to hold my own at that weight. I was 6ft 2in, so he was sure that I would develop into a fully fledged heavyweight given time. Once I was around 14 stone, when I was heavy enough to fight with the heavyweights, he wanted to keep me at that weight. From his own experience he knew that dieting was not always beneficial to a fighter. He had fought as a lightweight during his career but he could easily have boxed at light-welterweight. Taking off that weight had caused him to be dehydrated in his later fights and, in turn, that led to his losing fights he might otherwise have won. That was a mistake he didn't want to repeat as a trainer.

Heavyweights have always been much more interesting than cruiserweights, and both Barry and Freddie wanted me to fight with the big boys. It wasn't really about money for any of us because, while heavyweights can earn a lot more, even at that weight Barry wasn't paying me very much. That said, he always made sure I had enough to get by, and if I needed anything bigger he would give me an advance on my next pay packet. Matchroom was like a family for me in that way, and I always thought that Barry liked to look upon me as a little boy.

That family feeling continued after I had left Matchroom. I met Barry once after my second child, Haley, had been born, and I told him all about her. Barry hadn't realised that I had kids and seemed genuinely touched to know that I was now a father. Maybe in his eyes I had grown up; after leaving his nest I had become a man. 'Give your kids a cuddle for me!' he said.

Freddie and Barry built me up slowly but surely, making sure that I didn't develop too fast. I would be fighting every two or three months against a mixed bag of opponents. Some of the guys I fought had decent records while others were just bums I knocked out easily.

Eddie Gonzalez, for example, whom I met when we travelled over to Hamburg for my first foreign outing, should have been a tough opponent. In two of his previous three fights he had gone the distance with both Larry Holmes and Riddick Bowe. He was never going to win against fighters of this quality, but he had been able to give them a good workout. I blew him away in the second round.

Two fights later, in January 1992, I had my first encounter in front of my home crowd, and there was a title on the line to boot! Norwich Sports Village was packed as I challenged Conroy Nelson, a big Canadian by way of Jamaica, for the vacant WBC International heavyweight title. I was so nervous because this was my biggest fight so far and the local press were watching my every move; but at the same time I was supremely confident.

People can say what they like about belts like this being worthless but, to me, it meant the world. Chris Eubank had held the same title in his division before challenging Nigel Benn for the middleweight championship, so nobody could tell me that it wasn't an important stepping stone in my career. Within the past year Nelson had lasted nine rounds with Smokin' Bert Cooper, who at that time was a decent heavyweight, so when I stopped him in the second round it showed everybody just how good I was. The atmosphere was brilliant and, as I won, the place erupted. The crowed were singing, 'We want Bruno! We want Bruno!' and I believed that I could have beaten big Frank there and then. I actually heard that Barry offered Bruno £500,000 to fight me but, sadly, nothing ever came of it.

The matchmaker for the next one should have been fired. We went all the way over to Amsterdam to meet Percell Davis, who was nothing more than 250lb of American blubber. There was no way I couldn't beat him and, sure enough, he went down in the first round. This was the kind of fight that was bad for business. In

Matchroom

America, mismatches of this sort count for nothing, but in Europe the fans are more discerning. Nigel Benn, who was with Matchroom at the time, said to me, 'Your last fight was so good, and then this. Why?' He was right to be upset because my career had been moving up a gear and I didn't need to be involved in this sort of farce.

During the week I would work very hard in the gym but on Fridays I always looked forward to going home. When I returned to Norwich I would usually take the train. Matchroom would give me the money I needed so that I could go and buy my ticket. There was a guy at Matchroom called Dave who thought that I was asking for too much, and to prove it he insisted on buying the ticket himself one week. I didn't think anything of it. If they didn't believe me, that was their problem – he was welcome to queue up for it as far as I was concerned. I took the ticket from him without even looking at it and caught my train as usual.

An old friend of mine was on the train that day so we sat chatting until the ticket collector came. What I didn't realise was that my ticket was actually valid from Romford to Lowestoft, meaning that I was on the wrong train. The collector spotted this and told me that I would have to pay the fare again. My friend knew that the guy was just doing his job, and offered to pay for me, but I was convinced that he was trying to rip me off. I didn't believe that the ticket was wrong and I started shouting at him. In the end he walked off, probably worried that I would attack him if he continued to argue with me.

Nothing But Trouble

When he had gone, my friend looked at me and said, 'Man, you never took shit from anybody, did you?' He was right, but after that I always bought my own tickets.

Following a lay-off of six months, I returned to Norwich to defend my WBC International title, and to put things right for the Percell Davis fight. My opponent was Jean Chanet, the French heavyweight, who had also been European champion. By the time I faced him he had already lost that title to Lennox Lewis, but he was still an awkward opponent. My combination punching was superb, and I made his eye blow up in the first round, but he just wouldn't give in. I was battering away at him round after round until finally, in the eighth, he'd had enough. Our neighbour, Steve, was sitting close to the ring and he told me, 'Herbie, this guy only lost the title a few months back. You're a class above.'

Chanet was tough, but nothing would ever compare to my next fight when we travelled over to Antwerp to meet Craig Petersen from Australia. I had heard that aboriginal Australians were hard but I never expected anything like this guy. He gave me the hardest fight of my whole career, bar none. I was careless at the start of the fight and he punished me for it. My chin was high and he caught me with a hard hook to my jaw. It was a shock and I went down for the first time in my career. Even worse, he knocked my wisdom teeth out with that punch. If you look closely at the film of the fight you will be able to see pieces of those teeth on my lips. I was spitting them out, or swallowing them if they got lodged in my throat.

He was magnificently conditioned and just wouldn't stop fighting. I was so tired afterwards because he had applied so much pressure, but in the end I got the better of him in the seventh round.

A party had been organised for after the show but I didn't go. The pain in my jaw, where he had knocked out my teeth, was so intense that I felt I could do nothing. As well as this, I had such a severe headache that I just lay on my bed in the hotel room and prayed to God that he would take my life – it was the only relief I could imagine from this discomfort.

Craig and I met in the lift of the hotel the next morning, but such was the damage to his features that I didn't recognise him. 'You look like you had a hard fight,' I said to him, thinking he must have appeared in one of the other fights. 'Who did that to you?'

He thought that I was trying to wind him up. The worst of the bruising occurs after the fight and by now both of his eyes were swollen shut. He looked a real mess, and nothing like the guy who had been standing in the opposite corner 12 hours earlier.

It took about two weeks before I could eat normally again. I would go to my Auntie Winnie's house in Norwich and she would make the same food I would normally eat, such as vegetables and meat, so that I would still get my vitamins, and then put it in the blender. I would drink it with a straw, like a milkshake, until I could move my jaw again.

Craig was only 26 when he died in 1997, less than 5 years after our fight. He was found in his house in New Mexico after taking a drug overdose. It was a sad loss.

I collected another belt, this time the WBA Pentacontinental heavyweight title, when I beat Juan Antonio Diaz in the third round in Brentwood. He had been a decent amateur, even representing Argentina at the Seoul Olympics, but I did a job on him. It was my last fight before challenging for the British title.

Chapter 4

Me and my Minder

After leaving the house in Brentwood I moved into the Romford Villa, a huge house that Barry used to accommodate many of his boxers. There were a lot of us there, each with his own bedroom, although we had to share the kitchen and the bathroom.

I lived in the house with some well-known boxers, people such as Paul Busby, Eamonn Loughran, Shaun Cummins and Steve Collins. It was actually a nice house and I liked being there, but the boxers didn't keep it clean. We even had a cleaning lady but that made no difference. Can you imagine ten guys all using the same toilet and shower, and leaving plates all over the kitchen?

The guy I got along best with there was Francis Ampofo, the little fighter I had met at the ABA semi-finals a couple of years earlier. People would call us Twins, after the film of that name with Arnold Schwarzenegger and Danny DeVito (nothing like twins, obviously). We would do everything together, looking so funny because I was that much bigger than he was. Other than that, people would always refer to us as each other's minder. This wasn't far off the truth. I would stop any harm coming his way, and he would make sure that I didn't get into trouble.

Francis originally came from Ghana but he moved to London with his family when he was a kid, spending his youth in Bethnal Green in the East End. He is four years older than me but still joined the professional ranks slightly later than I did. He beat me to the British title though, winning it in only his seventh fight in 1991.

We used to wind each other up all the time when we were training. I would call him an 'Uncle Tom', just as Muhammad Ali did to Joe Frazier, which would really annoy him. I remember when he chased me through Romford market once, trying to hit me with a plank.

It was always so important for us to out-do each other, especially when it came to running. Over shorter distances he had no chance against me – I was much too fast. He was better at longer distances and would sometimes beat me. Once, after we'd had a big argument, Barry Hearn's son, Eddie, organised a race for us. I was much quicker than Francis and started running backwards so that I could look at him chasing me. All the while I was shouting, 'Come on, Uncle Tom! Come on, Uncle Tom!' He always thought he was fitter than I was, but he couldn't catch me on this occasion.

All of that was normal for us. We were living in each other's pocket and sometimes we would bicker. Even so, Francis is one of my best friends in the whole world. He even asked me to be the godfather of his eldest daughter, Olivia – the only person ever to crap on me. She was a year old and we were all on holiday together in Gran Canaria when I made the mistake of holding her while she didn't have her nappy on – I needed to take a long shower after that to recover.

Although I had collected a couple of belts by now, they carried little in the way of credibility. While they were important to me when I won them, I have to admit that titles like these are designed to enable an organisation such as the World Boxing Council (WBC) or the International Boxing Federation (IBF) to levy a sanctioning fee on the promoter, who in turn can sell a 'championship' fight to the public. Everybody makes money, not least the television companies, who care more about offering the illusion of quality than providing worthwhile boxing matches.

The British title, on the other hand, is steeped in tradition. Since it was introduced by the Earl of Lonsdale in 1909 as a prize for the champion in each weight division in Great Britain, there have been many illustrious holders of the gold and porcelain belts. In the heavyweight division, everybody who is anybody has had the honour of being called champion. Henry Cooper, Brian London, Joe Bugner and Lennox Lewis all held the title during their careers.

My opportunity came in February 1993, when I was still only 21. Lennox had been the previous champion but he had vacated the title several months earlier in order to pursue his world championship ambitions. I was to contest the championship with the Manchester heavyweight, Michael Murray.

At first, the British Boxing Board of Control were

unhappy about allowing Murray to challenge for the title. He had lost 4 of his 15 fights and, while that didn't mean he was a bum, the Board felt that he wasn't of a high enough standard for a championship fight. For this reason they refused to sanction the bout, but after Barry went back to them they agreed to let it go ahead.

It was also around this time that boxing insiders started to mention me as a future opponent for Riddick Bowe. I didn't take much notice because he held two of the major heavyweight titles and was regarded as the best of all the champions – even though he had dumped his WBC belt in a rubbish bin rather than defend it against Lennox Lewis – while I was still a comparative novice. It seemed very unlikely that I would be granted a fight against somebody like Bowe at this stage of my career. Anyway, he arrived at ringside at the Goresbrook Leisure Centre in Dagenham with his wife, Judy, who fell asleep during the fight, and his manager, Rock Newman, to give me the once-over.

Murray was the Central Area heavyweight champion when we met – Central Area referring to central England rather than his midriff, although he did look a bit podgy around the belly. Despite his holding this belt, he was the kind of guy who could make a bit of money by working as a sparring partner but who was never going to crack the big time. Actually, he had been working as my sparring partner four weeks before the fight.

I was still a cruiserweight, even though I was fighting in the heavyweight division. I never had any fear of facing bigger men – Freddie King always used to tell me that, if you're better than the other guy, size doesn't matter – but being so small was still a bit embarrassing for me. On the day of the weigh-in I told Francis Ampofo that I didn't want to go. Of course, I had no choice if I wanted to fight for the title, but I waited until the onlookers had left and then let them weigh me when I was by myself. The official weight was 14st 4lb but in reality I weighed in at 13st 3lb, more than a stone lighter. I never had a problem making the cruiserweight limit but Barry and Freddie wanted me to fight as a heavyweight, and I was happy to oblige.

I already knew from our sparring sessions what kind of guy Michael Murray was. When he first came to work with me at Matchroom he saw that I was a smaller heavyweight and after that he fancied his chances, a bit like a bully who is picking on somebody smaller than himself. I may not have looked as if I could trouble him but, once I landed a couple of punches and showed him how much strength I had in my fists, he quickly lost heart.

It was pretty much the same when we met in Dagenham. At first he believed that he could do a number on me but, after I rushed at him in the first round and landed a couple of hurtful blows, he backed off for the rest of the fight. Don't forget, the pressure was on me to impress the public and not on Michael. It was OK for him to go into survival mode and do nothing because nobody was expecting him to go on to better things. I was forced to go looking for him, unleashing my punches where I could, and he was making me look silly.

He hurt me in the first round, but I floored him in every subsequent session until the referee stopped it in the fifth. He clung to the ropes and I hammered him for virtually the whole fight.

Nothing But Trouble

This certainly wasn't my best ever performance but the criticism I received from the media afterwards was ridiculous. They called my performance amateurish, saying that I was nowhere near to world level and that I didn't deserve a shot at Riddick Bowe. I was only 21 and this kind of criticism was new to me. Today I would ignore it – many of these critics don't know what they are talking about anyway – but back then it really hurt. I drove home that evening in my new BMW as the new British heavyweight champion and I was crying my eyes out. How could these people be saying these things about me after all I had achieved?

Mickey Duff got wind that I didn't have a passport and started asking questions about whether or not I was a Nigerian and therefore unfit to fight for the British title. Later, when he saw my dad – a white Englishman – he stopped asking questions. The reason I didn't have a passport was that I hadn't needed one. As a kid my parents had one and I travelled on theirs. Any other time I had needed to leave the country, which wasn't very often, I had been able to get the necessary paperwork together without having to apply for a full passport. It was just something that I hadn't got round to doing, although that didn't mean I wasn't qualified to fight for the British title.

The thing with Mickey is that he's been in the trade a long time and he has a very astute business mind. He was managing Henry Akinwande at the time and he wanted to force a fight between the pair of us. Henry won the Commonwealth heavyweight title shortly after I won the British belt, and a fight between us made sense, at least to Mickey. Outside the ring Henry is a lovely fella, and even now I still have a lot of time for him, but his problem is that he's the sort of fighter people don't want to watch, and whom boxers don't want to fight. He's tall and unexciting, and his rangy style will make you look bad because it's so difficult to fight against him. Because of this he wasn't commanding much money and Mickey was only doing his job and trying to raise Henry's profile. Even so, it was a fight we didn't want. We just felt that Henry had everything to gain and that he wouldn't be bringing enough money to the table to make it worth my while.

Something that did show there were people who appreciated my achievement, and who acknowledged that I had done something to put Norwich on the map, took place in the days following the fight, when Les King organised a reception for me with the Lord Mayor, Councillor Arthur Clare, and the Lady Mayoress, Mrs Zaharat Power-Clare. A police escort accompanied a chauffeur-driven white Rolls-Royce, where I sat in the back with Freddie King and Les King, and Barry's limousine carrying Les's wife, among others, and with Barry's driver Robbo at the helm, as we travelled from Les's Regal Cinema to the City Hall.

Inside the City Hall we were met by the Lord Mayor and Lady Mayoress, who showed us to the Mancroft Room, where the guests were waiting to greet us. I had been allowed to invite 50 guests in all, and those included members of my family, friends from the Lads' Club and people I used to go to school with. Ronnie and Stephanie Brookes, Sean King, Dick Sadd and Chris Scott were just a few of those in attendance. It was a wonderful afternoon, which showed me how much my achievement meant to those close to me.

Now that I was the British champion I had a bit more money in my pocket than before. Don't get me wrong, I still wasn't rich, but my stock had risen and so had the purses. You wouldn't know it to look at me though. I would still walk around in my training gear, like the time I tried to buy a watch in a jeweller's shop. Francis Ampofo had been walking down the street with me, dressed just as casually as I was, when we passed a shop window displaying TAG Heuer watches. This was just what I had been looking for, so we went inside so that I could try one on for size. The owner of the shop refused to hand it over to me. He said that before he would let us try anything on we needed to show him our passports. I couldn't believe this guy. Here I was, the British heavyweight champion, and he was telling me that I needed to identify myself so that I could try on a watch that cost no more than a few hundred pounds – let's not forget, this wasn't a Rolex.

'What's the matter with you?' I yelled at him. 'Don't you think I can afford this? Well, I can afford it. Easily.'

Francis sensed that I would probably have dragged him over the counter if I had stayed in the shop any longer, so he ushered me outside before things turned nasty. As I have already said, he's my minder when I get into situations like this. That man missed out on a customer that day – more fool him.

All of these little troubles were put into perspective when my younger brother, Alan, was diagnosed with leukaemia. My parents had known that something was wrong with him but the doctors in Nigeria were not able to find anything. When they brought him over to England for some tests we found out exactly how ill he was. Even though this was a shock for all of us, I was still not too worried. He was going to get the treatment he needed and recover. Nothing and nobody could hurt him, especially with an older brother who was going to be the heavyweight champion.

But there was also newfound happiness in my life. My parents had sold the house in Chingford and had moved their British home over to Eaton, which was close by and slightly nearer to the centre of Norwich. That was where I met Helen for the first time and we became an item. She was the kind of girlfriend I wanted. When you are well known, especially in a small city like Norwich, there are always plenty of women who are interested in you, but those weren't the kinds of girls I was looking for. I wanted somebody with a bit more class, who was more down to earth and sensible, and who wasn't taken in by my celebrity status. Helen was just that kind of girl and, even now, all these years later, we are still together.

It's sad that I never managed to defend the British title. My plan had been to make a couple of quick defences and claim permanent possession of the Lonsdale Belt in double-quick time, but it never worked out that way.

A defence had been lined up against Clifton Mitchell, the unbeaten but inexperienced heavyweight from Derby, who trained under Brendan Ingle at the Wincobank Gym in Sheffield. He had already beaten Michael Murray and had sat at ringside with Naseem Hamed as I won the title, shouting, 'Fight me next!'

Barry was already on good terms with Brendan Ingle,

Clifton's manager, and he invited him into my dressing room afterwards, agreeing that I would fight Clifton in my first defence. The deal was done, or so I thought. Clifton suddenly didn't want to know, claiming that there was not enough time for him to prepare for the fight. I thought that he was a nice guy, but a real pussy.

In the end I had to pursue other options and, less than three months after claiming the British title, I was again in the ring, back in Norwich, where I faced Jerry Halstead. He was a very experienced campaigner from the US, having fought about 90 times. Most of his fights had taken place on small shows in his home state of Oklahoma but he had been in with some bigger-name fighters as well, losing to the likes of James Douglas, Greg Page and Ray Mercer before I fought him.

My confidence was very low going into the fight. The criticism from the Murray fight had affected me quite deeply and I needed a great performance to reassure myself that I was as good as I believed I was. It didn't help that the crowd in Norwich Sports Village weren't as enthusiastic as they had been when I had won the WBC International title over a year earlier. The problem was, I believe, that I had become too big for them. Chris Eubank once told me something that still rings very true. His experience of coming up in a smaller city, Brighton in his case, was similar to mine in Norwich. He said, 'In order to be a hero you need to be humble and act as though you are below everybody. Otherwise they will hate you, Herbie.'

Knocking Halstead out in the fourth round did my ego some good, even if little else did that evening.

The pressure of being a knockout specialist was getting

to me a bit. I had won all of my first 22 bouts inside the distance and now people were expecting every fight to end early. When I met Everett Martin in Leicester the following September, I could have knocked him out if I had wanted to, but I chose to lay off a bit and win clearly by decision. I knocked him to the canvas in the first round and there were several points during the fight when I could have moved up a gear to bring an early end to the proceedings but, in the end, I chose to coast through the rounds. It proved to me, and to everybody watching, that I was more than just a knockout artist. I could box as well if I needed to.

Mike Dixon was a heavyweight who had already lost to many of the better fighters in the division, including Lennox Lewis, Bruce Seldon and Ray Mercer. I saw him live in Las Vegas in 1993 when he beat Alex Garcia in two rounds. There was something about him that I thought would be perfect for me, so I whispered to Barry, 'Can I fight this guy?' Sure enough, Barry brought him over to England for me the following November and we fought at the York Hall. He was very tough and I had to work hard, but I was eventually able to stop him in the ninth round.

For my last fight before the close of the year, and also my last one before I fought for a world title, I travelled over to Sun City in South Africa to meet Jeff Lampkin in December. This was a trip that really opened my eyes. Even though I had been born in Nigeria, and had spent the early years of my life there, what I saw during my two weeks in South Africa was nothing like what I had known in my home country.

One evening as I left my hotel room, I met two men in

the foyer who offered to show me the sights. The three of us travelled to see the Zinc Houses, otherwise known as shanty towns, where a lot of black South Africans still live, years after the end of apartheid. These weren't even houses – they were more like huts, built from corrugated metal. It really was the most dangerous area for a foreigner to be by himself. I looked at what I saw and just thought, 'What on earth is this?' It was more frightening than anything I had seen in Nigeria.

We went to a nightclub there, which was also a bit intimidating for me at first, but once people realised that I was a boxer they took to me. Thankfully, my two friends brought me back to my hotel afterwards.

Jeff Lampkin had been a top-level cruiserweight who had beaten Britain's Glenn McCrory in 1990 for the IBF championship. He was stripped of the title in 1991 and, since then, he had dropped a couple of decisions before meeting me for my WBC International title. I wanted to make a good impression before my world-title fight against Michael Bentt but it almost went wrong when Lampkin hit me after the bell to end the first round, and I retaliated by firing a left hand at him, which knocked him to the canvas. The referee deducted a point from me for that, but it was all academic, as I stopped Lampkin in the next round. I floored him three times in total during those three minutes, the last one from a right hand after I had been bombarding him with punches, and he failed to beat the referee's count.

After this, I felt that I was ready to take on the world!

Chapter 5

Normal for Norfolk

Norwich is different from other British cities. You would need to have lived there to understand what it's like. Perhaps it is because it is tucked away in East Anglia, isolated from other populated areas, that the people there think and behave the way they do.

The city has had a bit of a rough ride in the media. It has been portrayed as a rural backwater, influenced by the yokel characteristics for which Norfolk is famous. Steve Coogan's comic creation, Alan Partridge, is just one of a host of fictional examples that play on the stereotype that Norwich people are somewhat detached from modern life.

Some would say that Norfolk deserves its reputation for strange behaviour, and not just because of my antics. Delia Smith probably didn't help matters very much when, in February 2005, while she was the chair of our local football team, Norwich City, she addressed the crowd at half time in a Premier League game against Manchester City with the immortal words, 'A message for the best football supporters in the world: we need a twelfth man here. Where are you? Where are you? Let's be having you! Come on!' Needless to say, the club and the city became the butt of jokes all around the country after that well-intended, but embarrassing, outburst.

And then there are the stories which suggest that Norfolk is some kind of a redneck stronghold. There was the news about two empty-heads at a Bernard Matthews farm who were convicted of playing baseball with live turkeys. They were sentenced to 200 hours of community service at Norwich Magistrates' Court in September 2006.

But, as anybody who knows the area will tell you, the impression that Norwich people are uncultivated is wide of the mark. Perhaps it is the accent that makes them sound a bit gormless to outsiders. Whatever it is, I don't believe that the level of inbreeding in our corner of the country is any greater than it is anywhere else in the United Kingdom.

That said, I did once find myself on the receiving end of some perverse sexual behaviour as a youngster in Norwich. It happened during the summer holidays after I had completed my first year at Cawston College. One of the locals saw me arguing with some other boys one day as I was returning home from the Lads' Club. Somebody had called me a nigger and I got upset about it.

After the other lads had disappeared, I continued to make my way home when this man approached me and asked what we had been arguing about. I told him why I was annoyed and he said that I had been correct to stand up for myself. Then he started preaching to me about racial understanding and a tolerant society. It was the first time we had ever spoken.

While I was shy as a youth, I wasn't afraid of anybody. I was a big, powerful lad and I believed that I could look after myself. It's probably for this reason that I let my curiosity get the better of me, accepting his invitation to follow him indoors. He then offered me some apple juice, which, for somebody who spent most of his time in a boarding school, was a real treat. At the same time he fixed himself a drink, although I wasn't really sure what it was, let me finish mine and then asked, 'Would you like another?'

'Yes, OK.'

'Why don't you try some of this?' he said. 'It's apple juice, like you've just been drinking, but a bit stronger.' He was offering me cider. I was 14 at the time and I hadn't tried alcohol before. It tasted a bit funny but, since he was talking to me as if I were an adult and I was enjoying the attention, I drank it anyway. It gave me a bit of a buzz as I felt the alcohol taking effect.

When he told me that he was involved in teaching sport I sat up and took notice. I was keen to show off about my sporting achievements. We carried on talking for a while, with him telling me that he knew a lot about rugby himself, and all the while I was getting more and more drunk.

'I'd like to show you some exercises we use,' he told me. This sounded interesting because I had trained under some good sport teachers and I was always keen to learn more. I got off the sofa and knelt on the floor.

'No, not like that,' he said. 'I want you to lie on the floor.'

I had never seen an exercise like this before, but I did as he asked me. Then he sat on top of me and took my hands in his, interlocking his fingers with mine. Alarm bells were starting to ring in my head because this didn't feel at all right. He started to gyrate his groin, sitting right on top of my dick. Then he tried to kiss me.

At that point I pushed him off and ran outside. I was shocked and confused by the whole experience, and I didn't know what to do. I was still a virgin and I didn't know the first thing about *heterosexual* sex, never mind this sort. If a *girl* had tried to kiss me at that age I would have panicked, so having a grown man try it really upset me.

I went home and told my mum about it and she became hysterical, crying her eyes out. Of course, she was worried that he may have done other things that I wasn't telling her about and it took me a while before I could convince her that it hadn't got that far. My mum called my Auntie Winnie, who said that we must make a statement to the police right away.

For the first few days afterwards I was traumatised. I couldn't sleep alone, so I would stay in my mum's room during the night. Eventually the shock eased, but it was a horrible experience.

My mum told a neighbour of ours, a lady called Janet, what had happened to me but she wouldn't believe it at first. She just said something along the lines of, 'I don't think he's like that.'

To me it felt as if she thought I was making the whole thing up. I would pray that our local pervert would get his hands on her son, Stuart, just to prove her wrong. Within a few weeks she had changed her tune anyway, telling my mum, 'He's definitely a funny man.' Everybody in the village was coming to realise that. The sad thing is the police went to see him about it but they couldn't do anything. It was my word against his and he wasn't about to admit to abusing boys.

The thing with Norwich people is that they feel much better when they can look down on you. I never had the feeling that people there were prejudiced against me because of my colour. When I first arrived, there were very few Africans or West Indians in Norwich and even now the proportion of black people is very low in comparison with, say, London or Birmingham. But that was never a reason for the local people to view me with suspicion or distaste. My initial reception there was quite friendly. As long as I knew my place, people did not feel threatened by me. As I grew older, and as I took to boxing, people would be happy to encourage me. That changed when I started making a name for myself further afield.

Maybe my wealth and fame were a bit difficult for many people to accept. I had been a very shy, inhibited youngster who stuttered and kept himself to himself. The only place I would ever show any form of confidence was in the boxing gym or on the rugby pitch, away from the eyes of many of the locals. I was never one of them, but I didn't do them any harm either, so they were happy to let me go about my business in peace. As I became successful my name was constantly in the media and I started to outgrow the city. Norwich is like a goldfish bowl in that way. There aren't many celebrities in Norfolk, and those who do become famous are already known by everyone who lives there.

Chris Scott once told me, 'You can't stay here, Herbie. They'll hate you.' In hindsight I now know what he meant. Norwich is a graveyard for success. There are certain people who, rather than take a pride in a local boy who has made good, prefer to knock him off his pedestal. There are those who will argue that I never did make good, that I am just a thug with a big house, but there is nothing I can do to convince those people. As long as the police in Norwich have a bone to pick with me then the local people will tend to believe what they hear.

The Norfolk boys in blue have had it in for me for a long time. There never used to be a problem but, once I started building my mansion at Bawburgh, they obviously thought that I was getting above my station. It's a funny thing because the Lads' Club in Norwich, the club that set me on my path to becoming a world champion, was actually set up by a police officer who wanted to promote a better understanding between the police force and the local youths. So, in a way, they helped to make me what I am, and it's what I am now that they object to.

It may seem strange coming from somebody who might as well hold a season ticket at the Norwich police station, but before 1992 I had never even been arrested. There is a first time for everything though, and when it happened it was a lot of fuss about nothing. I was the holder of the WBC International Belt, so I was quite well known locally and maybe this is why the incident drew more attention than it should have, but I hadn't made any real money yet, so the locals had nothing to be envious of. I had arranged for my keys to be sent on to me in Norwich after I had left them in Romford. I owned a dog at the time and he was stuck in the house, so I needed to let myself in so that I could see to him. The staff at Matchroom arranged to send the keys over to me on the next train and that would have been fine. I had been to see Les King after arriving back and we went to the station together to pick them up. The problem was that they had been mislaid somewhere, meaning that I would need a locksmith to open the door.

Mistakes can happen but I didn't see that I should be the one to foot the bill for the locksmith, so I asked who was going to pay. Nobody at the station could help me, so they called a customer-relations officer in Manchester for me. He was actually a very rude man who told me quite bluntly that British Rail were not responsible for the locksmith, only for the key itself, and that, if I filled out the forms, I would be reimbursed. That really got on my nerves, so I started screaming down the phone at him. How much does a key cost? Fifty pence? I slammed down the receiver and accidentally knocked a computer off a desk. That was when they called the police, and so began a long and beautiful relationship. It was my first arrest – not very gangster-like at all. I also had to pay for the computer to be replaced.

But, for all that, I have some very good friends in Norwich. There's a funny guy called Steve I met in the hospital when I was having my hand fixed. It was a stage I was going through where I would be training during the day and then letting my aggression spill out onto the streets in the evening. There was nothing really bad about what I was doing. I just had too much energy and would get a bit rowdy sometimes. When I broke my thumb it was Steve who fixed it. He asked me how I did it, but he knew precisely what had happened and then went on to tell me off for brawling. His face was familiar to me from somewhere, but I just couldn't place him. He knew who I was though, and he knew that I had a bit of a reputation as a rebel. He had seen me at my parents' house in Eaton, which was close to where he lived.

Every time I went back to that hospital it would be the same old story: Steve would fix me up and tell me off, and after a while we got to know each other very well. He would always have a good laugh at my expense when my parents had been in England and my mum went shopping for food to take back to Africa. I was the one who would be asked to unload the black cab, which by then resembled a Red Cross lorry, while she paid the driver. Watching me lug all that food into the kitchen so that it could all be packed into suitcases was terrific entertainment for Steve.

He also thought I was a DIY disaster, never letting me forget the time I went round to borrow his drill. All I wanted to do was hang up a picture in my parents' house but Steve had to step in and help me when I couldn't work out how to use it.

His wife, Jackie, is probably the most house-proud woman in Norfolk. When you go to their house you are expected to take off your shoes before you enter the living room, no matter how rich or famous you might be. She always seems to have a duster in her hand whenever I'm there, and she loves telling Steve off. I go around checking for dust just to see if she has missed something.

I think Steve is under Jackie's thumb, but in the nicest possible way. They met while he was playing rugby. He took her number, made a date, and she put down the phone on him. Even back then she was showing him who was the boss. They are both lovely people though, as are their kids. They are just the kind of people who make me feel that Norwich is my home.

Chapter 6

Rolling in Puddles

Few outside the boxing fraternity had heard of Michael Bentt at the beginning of 1993. He had enjoyed an outstanding amateur career, winning all but 8 of his 183 unpaid fights, but after turning professional with Emanuel Steward in Detroit in 1989 he had a disastrous debut: an ex-con called Jerry Jones knocked him out in the first round.

Michael was understandably disillusioned with the sport and took a couple of years out after that first fight. When he returned he reeled off ten consecutive victories but was still very much an anonymous face to many fight fans, who at that time were more familiar with heavyweights such as Mike Tyson and Evander Holyfield.

Nobody could have foreseen that events would unfold as they did, or that Michael's name would become inextricably linked with mine. In fact, if it hadn't been for Tommy Morrison, the Oklahoma tough guy who had appeared in the fifth *Rocky* film, Michael and I might never have even met. Tommy had beaten George Foreman in June 1993 to claim the vacant World Boxing Organisation (WBO) heavyweight title. The decision had been unpopular, but that didn't matter to Tommy and his followers, who were able to look forward to a proposed mega-fight in 1994 against Lennox Lewis, who held the WBC championship at the time. Against the wishes of his management, Tommy wanted to have a warm-up fight before he went head to head with Lennox. Clearly, they needed a relatively safe opponent – somebody who could fight a bit but who was unlikely to jeopardise the $7.5 million pay packet he would collect for the fight with Lennox. Michael was the perfect candidate and was chosen as Tommy's opponent for the fight, which took place in October 1993. He knocked Tommy down 3 times on the way to a 93-second victory.

A couple of names were mentioned as possible opponents for Michael's first defence, including Frank Bruno and George Foreman but, fortunately, I was chosen as his challenger. The fight was organised for 19 March at the New Den, the home of Millwall Football Club – supposedly Michael's favourite football team.

Rightly or wrongly, Michael claimed to be British. He was born in London, but when he was six he left to live in Jamaica, and then New York. I think most people would have looked at him as an American, but it was still a good angle to sell the fight. The year before, Lennox Lewis had beaten Frank Bruno in an all-British affair, so this was the second heavyweight title fight to feature two British fighters in a matter of months.

Barry organised a press conference at the Sheraton Park Tower Hotel in Knightsbridge to announce the fight in January, a couple of months before the event, and that was when I met Michael for the first time. He was already in the room when I arrived so I went over to him, shook his hand and thanked him for giving me this opportunity. Michael is a devout Muslim and he was surrounded by his Muslim bodyguards, who looked quite intimidating, although Michael was fine and he told me that he was glad to be in England.

I knew something about Michael that most other people wouldn't have noticed. He was able to hide it very well but it didn't escape me when I heard him speak. 'There's something we both share,' I told him. 'We both stutter.'

He was surprised that I had noticed but he didn't deny it. 'That's what makes us true warriors,' he replied after a moment or two. That was first blood to Herbie!

Something I found a bit daft was Michael's support for Millwall. He came to the press conference wearing a supporter's cap but, as everybody knows, the club has suffered from having a number of racist fans in the past. Michael, like me, was a black man so I couldn't really see what appealed to him about Millwall. I didn't really believe that he knew very much about football. 'Michael claims to be a Millwall supporter,' I told the press, 'but he probably thinks Pele plays for England.'

I was showing him that I could take the piss just as well as his people could. His trainer, Eddie Mustafa Muhammad, was one of the worst. It seems strange now, especially after Eddie and I struck up such a good relationship later in my career, but I didn't like him at all then. He came across as being extremely arrogant and disrespectful, telling everybody that Michael would easily beat me. The Americans are the best in the world at trash talking, putting the opponent down before the fight, but they don't expect it as much from the British fighters. I proved to them that I could fight fire with fire.

Things got really interesting when we went outside onto the hotel balcony for a photo shoot. Michael still had his Millwall cap on so I said to him, 'Why are you still wearing that daft hat, Michael? If you want to wear that then I want a Norwich City one.' With that I knocked it off his head.

I was only playing, but he obviously didn't think it was a game. Without any kind of warning he punched me, knocking me to the floor. He wasn't going to get away with that so I jumped on top of him and started hitting him back. We landed in a puddle and while I was on top of him he grabbed my balls. I couldn't do anything. He squeezed so hard that I had to surrender. What else could I have done? I had never felt anything like that before in my life. The pain was indescribable and for the next week my gonads were numb – I had to play with myself just to be sure that everything still worked.

Throughout all of this he still had his army of Muslim bodyguards behind him while I was on my own. Yes, I knew quite a few people who were there but nobody was about to fight my corner for me. I weighed up the situation for a few seconds and then went back inside to find an ashtray so that I could whack him over the head. When I came back outside I was carrying this beautiful, heavy, marble ashtray, which would have been perfect for smacking Michael with, when Barry stepped in and grabbed my wrist. After that, things died down a bit and we all left, but that scuffle had instilled a hatred of Michael in me that would remain until the day of the fight.

Both Michael and I were fined £10,000 for that by the British Boxing Board of Control. John Morris, the Board's secretary, even went as far as to label us 'two stupid young men'. I didn't think it was fair, but that's boxing politics for you. For one thing, Michael threw the first punch. For another, as champion he was earning about six times as much as I was so, relatively speaking, I was made to suffer more. In any case, Barry paid my fine for me, but I still thought that the Board had a cheek.

My share of the purse was about £100,000. It's a bit annoying when you hear that the other guy is getting something like £600,000, but I was still getting more than I had ever earned before – it was a major step up financially for me. When I first turned professional I was getting £500 each time I featured in a fight, so this felt like a different world to me. Of course, Michael didn't tell me what he was paid for the fight, but I was able to find out when I read the papers. The reporters are good at finding out about purses. One of their tricks is to call the Board, ask how much commission they are getting from the fight and then do the maths.

Whatever the Board thought of this little episode, at least somebody had been impressed by my performance. Jimmy McDonnell, who was working with Freddie King, my trainer, as my conditioner and motivator, saw me the next morning and said, 'You killed him yesterday, now you have to kill him again.'

Sky TV had organised a charity basketball event to take place in London in the early part of 1994 and I was glad to be invited to play because it showed me that my name was now becoming well known in sporting circles. Several football stars, people such as Ian Wright and David Seaman, were signed up, as were Kriss Akabusi and Lennox Lewis. Francis Ampofo came along with me to see the game, although he wasn't asked to play – he was much too small.

As we sat in the back of the Matchroom limo, with Robbo chauffeuring us from Romford to London, Francis said to me, 'You know what, Herbie? You're going to be the best heavyweight ever. I think you could beat Lennox Lewis.'

That made me feel so happy. I was over the moon that Francis thought that way and it really motivated me for the evening ahead. Francis was like that, but not in a bum-licking kind of way. He would just tell people what he thought they wanted to hear. Maybe it was because he was so small and he was just happy people would listen to him at all.

He loved attention, even though he received less public recognition as a flyweight than I did as a heavyweight. That's life – the bigger guys have always been more interesting. We were walking down the street together once when somebody stopped him and asked if he was Francis Ampofo, the British flyweight champion. He was absolutely made up that this man had noticed him. When the guy came back past us in the opposite direction a few minutes later, Francis insisted that they have their photo taken together. Can you imagine that? The celebrity pestering the fan for a picture? He wanted to show it to everyone as proof that people recognised him. I bet he still has it filed away somewhere now.

Rolling in Puddles

After we finished the basketball game we got talking to some of the other players. Francis didn't realise it at the time, but I was listening in as he was talking to Lennox Lewis. 'You're the best Lennox,' I heard him say. 'You'll beat all of them.'

This all sounded a bit different from what I had heard him say in the car a couple of hours earlier, so I thought it would be a good time to join in the conversation. 'Francis,' I said, 'that's not quite what you said in the limo earlier, is it? You said that Lennox is useless as a boxer and that he's probably gay.'

Lennox's face just dropped. I have to point out here that Lennox is not gay (we both dated the same girl once, although not at the same time) and Francis never even said he was – all he said was that I would beat him. I just thought it was funny to land him in some trouble with this huge guy after all he had said.

'No, no, I didn't,' Francis said, and walked off before I got him in any more bother.

Something similar once happened with Steve Collins. I had been out having breakfast with Francis at the local Little Chef when somebody approached me and asked what I thought was going to happen in the upcoming first fight between Steve and Chris Eubank.

'Steve Collins is lazy. He doesn't train and he's just in it for the money,' Francis piped in. 'Eubank will beat him easily.'

I hadn't taken too much notice and I said nothing more about it. My fight with Riddick Bowe was getting close and I was far more concerned with that than I was with Steve's next bout. That was until we got back to the Romford Villa and found Steve in the kitchen boiling potatoes.

Nothing But Trouble

'Hello, Steve,' said Francis in an overly friendly tone. 'How's it going? Are you ready for Eubank? I don't think you'll have any problems at all with him.'

'Francis,' I said. That was it. He knew what I was about to say and wanted to get out of the kitchen. 'Why don't you tell Steve what you said in the café? What was it you said?'

'Nothing,' he replied, just like a naughty schoolboy.

'Do you want me to tell him for you?' By this point Steve had lost interest in his potatoes and was watching us very closely.

'All I said was, if he doesn't train well, he might, just possibly . . .'

That was enough. Steve knew that he was lying and looked completely pissed off with Francis. Francis was annoyed with me for landing him in it and wouldn't talk to me for the best part of five minutes. He knows that I love embarrassing him.

Thanks to Jimmy, I went into the Bentt fight fitter than ever before. I trained so intensely for the fight, both in the gym and out on the streets, that I was in my best ever shape. The sparring with Buster Mathis Jr went perfectly, and Freddie was able to instil his battle plan brilliantly. Physically, I was in wonderful shape, with Jimmy overseeing my running, and mentally I had never felt better. I even had to ask Freddie why I wasn't nervous.

'You've trained so hard,' he told me. 'You know that you're going to win.'

Another press conference took place a few days before the fight. Of course, knowing what had gone on the last time, the press flooded the place. Barry stood in the middle as Michael and I were asked to shake hands, but then Michael said something to Barry and an argument ensued. I'm not really sure what was said but it had an effect on Barry, because he turned around to me and said, 'Herbie, I'm glad you're the one who's fighting him, and not me.'

Thanks, Barry! Just what I needed to hear right before the biggest fight of my life.

Neither of us really wanted to shake hands with each other, especially after what had happened at the first press conference, but Barry pulled us together. There was a lot of tension in the room, with a really bad atmosphere between us. I hated his guts at that point and he probably felt the same about me.

Again, Michael was surrounded by his Muslim bodyguards. These were serious-looking guys, just the kind of people you don't want to get on the wrong side of. They stood there with no emotion on their faces, wearing dark sunglasses even though we were indoors, watching every move. I told the press that we were at a Malcolm X lookalike contest, something these guys didn't find at all amusing. They just looked at me and raised their eyebrows.

Michael wasn't the only person to whom I had something to prove though: I wanted to show the whole British media that I was as good as I said I was. The amount of unfair criticism I had taken was unbelievable. People in the press were saying that I had beaten only bums, that I didn't have enough experience to fight for a world title, and that I wasn't all that good anyway. It's a British thing. The press love knocking their own people off their pedestals, no matter how talented they are. In my case, I could beat only the people who were put in front of me and I had done this easily. They may have been fighting at a lower level than I was, but that didn't mean I wasn't ready to step up in class. This was my chance to show everybody who had ever written something negative about me that I belonged with the elite fighters.

When I stepped out on that cold March evening I was booed from all sides. This was more like a football crowd than a boxing crowd, with the fans chanting, 'Millwall, Millwall' as I made my way to the ring. I knew why they didn't like me. After I knocked Michael's Millwall cap off they saw it as disrespect for their football team. You don't think about these things at the time, but football fans love their clubs and Michael had done much more than I had to gain their sympathy.

Young men, probably no older than I was, were trying to intimidate me with their chants. I had nothing against their team, but they weren't to know that and they were calling for my blood. I was only 22 years old and it might have bothered me but I turned it to my advantage. I told myself that *I* was the special one here, that these people who were booing me would never be special, as I was. They had paid to come in, all 10,000 of them, and they were helping to make this the most lucrative fight of my career.

We knew that Michael's right hand would be dangerous, especially after what he did to Tommy Morrison. That's why it was important to stay out of his way, keep moving, and pepper him with jabs from the outside. I danced around him faster than anything he had ever seen before. You cannot punch what you cannot see, and Michael was having real difficulty with me.

Rolling in Puddles

This went on for the first two rounds. My left jab was working beautifully, breaking through Michael's guard and forcing him back while my right-handers were catching him too. He came out a bit stronger in the third round, but then I caught him with a superb right uppercut, which knocked his head right back and sent him crashing to the canvas. When he rose I manoeuvred him into the corner and blasted away. All he could do was to turn his back on me, something for which the referee could have stopped the bout.

Michael sensed that he had no chance of beating me with his own boxing skills, so he started holding. At the end of the seventh I caught him with two hard rights to the head and he landed on his belly, even bouncing an inch or two off the canvass when he landed. That was the end of the show. He beat the count, just about, but Paul Thomas, the referee, called a halt before I could do any more damage. I had gone in there wanting to annihilate Michael, and I did just that.

Those fans who booed me on the way in were cheering for me now. Everybody was on my side as I took the microphone and thanked them for coming. 'Just so you know,' I told them, 'I have nothing against Millwall Football Club.' That was the truth. I was only playing when I knocked Michael's hat off; there was no disrespect intended to Millwall.

For the first time in my life I was the world champion, and there's no better feeling than that. Nothing can top the sensation of knowing that you have reached the pinnacle of your sport. You experience this kind of sensation only once. All my dreams had come true and, whatever happened after that, nobody could take away from me the fact that I had been a world champion. When I won the championship for the second time, three years later, it wasn't the same. That was for Alan. This one was for me.

I remember getting back to my dressing room and the place being flooded with people. I was dancing around, partying, and everybody there was just so happy for me. My mum and dad were in there, and Alan was at the centre of it all. We opened a bottle of champagne and then I went to have my shower. When I came out, wearing nothing but a smile, most of the people were still there. My mum told me to cover myself up.

We went to the press conference and – wouldn't you believe it? – there were journalists there who wanted to talk about how badly Michael had fought, rather than how I had just done Britain proud. They should have given me more credit but, unlike with the Michael Murray fight, I didn't let it get to me. As I have already said, you cannot beat what you cannot hit. That was the reason Michael looked so bad: he just couldn't get his punches to land. 'All my opponents always look as if they can't fight because they can't hit me,' I told them. Michael Bentt was no exception. He tried to hit me but I was too good for him. The press should have applauded me for that.

Going into that fight, I had been the underdog. People believed I was too young and too raw, that a fighter like Michael would know how to beat me. Now I was a world champion and the media had to accept that they had been wrong. 'I want you all to kneel down and kiss my arse,' I told them. 'I want you all to kneel down and say, "You're the greatest." Because I am.'

Rolling in Puddles

Michael didn't join us at the press conference. What we didn't know at the time was that he had collapsed in the dressing room shortly after the fight and had to be rushed to hospital in an ambulance. The doctors diagnosed a concussive brain injury and said that a CAT scan showed some swelling. They told him that his career as a prizefighter was finished and, sure enough, he never fought again.

When something like that happens to an opponent, a fighter must ask himself some questions. Is it something he can deal with? Does he feel guilty about it? There are boxers who find it very difficult to continue in the sport after somebody has been badly hurt. In my case it didn't have much of an effect on me. You have to remember that this was a grudge match and a lot of punches were flying. There was always a chance that somebody could have been injured and, as far as I am concerned, it could just as easily have been me. We fighters know the risks, even though most us believe that it will never happen to us, and things like this will occur from time to time. Thankfully, there was no tragedy. Michael may have been forced to retire, but he still lives a normal life. Perhaps if he had carried on boxing he would have been seriously hurt later on, but that never happened.

Fighters who lose are always ready to offer excuses. In Michael's case I have heard a few. One was that he was weakened through fasting for Ramadan. Another was that he had been knocked out in training by his sparring partner, King Ipitan. This is something I don't buy into because, whatever happens in sparring, it won't make much of a difference to the fight. Boxers are often knocked down, or knocked out, by sparring partners. It's a risk of the trade, although something like this would usually be covered up unless it happened in an open training session. I have been knocked down several times in sparring, but that didn't usually stop me from winning the fight. You are either good enough to win the fight or you aren't, and a sparring partner won't change that. It's no different from the knockout he suffered in his first fight. That was a bitter setback, but not one that was going to stop him from being a useful heavyweight. A decent heavyweight will recover from it and move on.

To be fair to Michael, he has since said that, even if those things hadn't happened before the fight, I would still have beaten him. I was just so good on the evening.

Nobody was going to take anything away from me after that victory. As we drove back to Norwich that night in Barry's limo, Nigel Brightwell sat beside me and we drank champagne all the way home. I was the new champion of the world and it felt amazing. This was the greatest night of my life.

Chapter 7

Hitting Vegas

My reign as heavyweight champion could not have got off to a more disappointing start. Barry Hearn, together with the American promoter Bob Arum, and John Daly, an American entrepreneur, had agreed to promote a show in Hong Kong – a show that fell apart at the very last minute. It was a particularly ambitious project, designed to pit four top British boxers against American counterparts. The promotion, as the title of 'High Noon in Hong Kong' suggests, was to take place around midday on 23 October 1994 and I had been billed for the main event, making it the first defence of my title against Tommy Morrison. In another big heavyweight clash, Frank Bruno was to make his long-awaited comeback against Ray Mercer, a year after losing to Lennox Lewis. Steve Collins, whom I knew from the Matchroom stable, had been booked to make a defence of his WBO middleweight belt and Luton's Billy Schwer was also slated to challenge Rafael Ruelas for the IBF lightweight championship.

Nothing But Trouble

Daly had helped Don King finance the 'Rumble in the Jungle' in 1974, where Muhammad Ali successfully dethroned the then heavyweight champion, George Foreman, in the Democratic Republic of the Congo (then called Zaïre). He owned a company called Hemdale Communications Inc., which had provided financing for a number of successful Hollywood films, and that was enough for Barry.

The Far East had been a lucrative market for the sport, with countries such as Japan and the Philippines boasting a number of world champions at lighter weights. Hong Kong was uncharted territory for a major boxing event and this promotion was intended to make a killing. The event was to be staged outdoors on Hong Kong Island, at the Hong Kong Stadium, in front of 40,000 paying spectators. At first it all sounded very promising.

My training camp was set up in Norwich, where Barry had organised a marquee at the Barnham Broom Hotel and Country Club. This took me back to the days before I fought for the British title, when I would visit Fitness Express, an onsite fitness centre there, virtually every day. A man there called Cefyn Lloyd helped me to add the muscle I needed to establish myself as a natural heavyweight. Fitness Express were again on hand, organising the training equipment in the marquee.

Steve Collins joined me at Barnham Broom. We were both trained by Freddie King at this time and, as Freddie had agreed to prepare me in my home city, Steve came too. Steve felt that, as the Matchroom gym was in Romford, we should have trained there, and that the fact that we were training in Norwich was another example of a heavyweight receiving preferential treatment. We both held the WBO championship in our respective weight divisions and Steve felt that his title was worth every bit as much as mine. It was clear to me that my belt was the more important of the two. For one thing, I was being paid over $1 million, while his purse was in the region of $50,000 – the trainer's fee is based on a percentage of what the fighter earns, so it made financial sense for Freddie to give me priority. For another, I was the headline act, while he was making up the undercard.

Something similar happened again in 1995 when I was preparing for my fight with Riddick Bowe, and Steve was getting ready for his first fight with Chris Eubank. Originally, Freddie and I had planned to train in Las Vegas and, as Steve also required Freddie's services, he decided to fly with us. The plans were later changed so that most of my preparation would take place in Romford. Even though he had been unhappy about travelling to Las Vegas in the first place, Steve decided to complete his training for the Eubank fight there anyway, without Freddie.

Steve had a very successful career, going on to outpoint Eubank in that fight for the WBO super-middleweight championship in Millstreet, Ireland, and again in a rematch in Cork, before stopping Nigel Benn twice in Manchester. However, while Eubank and Benn were stars in their own rights, Steve never really shared their charisma. He was never much of an attraction outside of his native Ireland but he will always be remembered in Britain, if only for fighting those two.

Before we left for Hong Kong I went out one night with Ian Allcock, my old mate from Brentwood, who was helping me with my preparation for the Morrison fight.

Nothing But Trouble

We'd been to a club in Norwich and were walking through the streets of the city when we ran into trouble with three young men. They weren't local boys – from their dialects it sounded as if they came from Liverpool – and they wanted to try their luck with us. I never go out looking for trouble, but when it comes my way I am always ready to deal with it. Things were about to turn nasty when one of them said in his Scouse accent, 'Erm, lads, I think we might be fucked here.'

'Why?' said another one.

'Because that black guy looks like Herbie Hide, the boxer.' With that, they all ran off. Talk about messing with the wrong person!

I was in Hong Kong for the two weeks leading up to the show and I didn't enjoy my time there at all. The place stank, the streets were packed with people and, if you tried crossing the road, you took your life in your hands. Then there was Frank Bruno. While I know many of the British heavyweights, Frank is somebody I had never really associated with. I had always had the impression that he didn't like me. When I was named Prospect of the Year in a ceremony at the Grosvenor House Hotel in London, Barry had asked him to present the award, but Bruno wasn't available. Frank has always been more than just a boxer. He's a media personality and he was supporting me on the bill in Hong Kong. He had already tried to win the heavyweight title three times by then and here I was, at 23 and already a world champion, stealing his thunder.

He did help me out though, when we were invited to meet Chris Patton, the Governor of Hong Kong before it reverted to Chinese rule, at his home in the city. Frank had been doing this kind of thing for years, while it was something new to me. He took charge of the questioning and made sure that I wasn't embarrassed.

Interest in the fight was nowhere near the level anticipated by John Daly. Ticket sales were disappointing, with only 8,000 seats 'sold' (rumour had it that half of those had been freebies) by the day of the event, and Daly found himself in serious financial difficulty. The promoters had been guaranteed over $1.5 million for staging the event and $800,000 of this had been obtained from his bankers in advance on the strength of the expected ticket sales and television revenue. When the ticket sales fell flat, the remainder of the guarantee, a sum totalling $771,000, was not forthcoming. At the eleventh hour Barry and Bob Arum decided to pull the plug on the entire show.

The cancellation of my fight and the loss of my purse didn't really bother me because I was still young and I had the world at my feet. My attitude was that the next fight would come and I would earn plenty of money then. It wasn't as if I really needed the cash, because I had no young family to support and no mortgage to pay. For other people it was different. Fighters such as Steve and Frank Bruno were a good few years older than I was and they couldn't afford to lose their earnings like this. I remember Frank being particularly despondent when he heard the news.

In a way I was quite relieved that the card would not go ahead. Two knuckles on my right hand had been injured in sparring and it was touch and go whether I could have fought anyway. It got to the stage where I really didn't fancy going through with the fight, and I imagine that I would have pulled out beforehand. I mentioned the injury to Barry but he said that it was best to keep quiet for the time being. I suppose he suspected that the promotion was on the verge of going belly up and that there was no point broadcasting the bad news if it was going to be irrelevant anyway. We left Hong Kong the day after the promotion should have taken place. I was glad to see the back of the place.

Frank Warren and Don King started making overtures to me around this time. As promoters they were still considered to be the dream team in professional boxing, King being the master who virtually controlled the sport in the US and Warren, his young apprentice, having many of the best fighters in Britain under contract. Warren had actually been to the gym in Norwich while I was still an amateur but he didn't want to sign me as a professional. I would have been 17 years old at the time and perhaps I was too raw for him. At 23, and as a holder of a world title, I was a much more polished performer and a much more attractive investment.

Frank Warren operates differently from Barry Hearn in the way he acquires his fighters. Barry will wait for fighters to come to him, while Warren sees what he wants and goes after it. In my case he did this by contacting John Hornewer, my adviser and friend, who in turn asked Jimmy McDonnell to organise the meeting. In football this would be known as 'tapping up', but in boxing anything is fair.

The venue was a McDonald's restaurant near the Old Bailey in London. There Jimmy and I met with Warren's solicitor, Steve Davis (not the snooker player), who made me a very lucrative offer. I was to receive around £20,000 upfront as a signing-on bonus, for which Warren would then have the promotional rights to my fights. Furthermore, if the WBO mandated that I must defend my title against Riddick Bowe, I would receive a guaranteed purse of about $4 million. I told Steve that I wanted some time to think it over and disappeared into the toilets.

Another meeting then took place with Warren himself, this time at his office in London. I had the impression that he didn't really want me to fight Bowe. He would have preferred less dangerous opponents so that I could move through the challengers, knocking out everybody and making a lot of money at each promotion. To seal the deal he called King in America and handed me the receiver.

You don't speak to Don King, you listen. It is impossible to get a word in edgeways when he is in full flow, so I let him continue for however long about his African brothers and how he always looked after his fighters. Maybe Warren thought that King's famed line in negro rhetoric would impress me but it didn't – it bored me. I waited for him to finish what he had to say and then said, 'Don, thank you, bye,' and with that I left Warren's office.

The fight with Riddick Bowe was finally organised for 11 March 1995, a year after I had last fought professionally. The venue was to be the MGM Grand in Las Vegas. Barry negotiated a very good deal for me whereby I was to receive $3.1 million and, in the event that Bowe won, $250,000 for each subsequent defence he made of the title. It was by far the biggest purse I had ever earned and would set me up for life.

Riddick, together with his manager Rock Newman, was looking to get back into the world-title picture. He was still one of the best heavyweights on the planet but his career had gone off the boil somewhat. A lot of it was his own fault. He didn't have the discipline he needed to control his food cravings and when he met Evander Holyfield for the second time, in November 1993, he was overweight and out of condition. Holyfield reclaimed the WBA and IBF belts that he had lost to Riddick in their first fight by dominating the action throughout. Even the arrival of a parachutist, who landed in the ropes during a bizarre stunt during the seventh round, wasn't going to help Riddick preserve his unbeaten record.

The WBC belt had also belonged to Riddick but he had dumped that in a rubbish bin rather than defend it against Lennox Lewis. Since then he had fought in two comeback fights. In the first he knocked out Buster Mathis Jr, an old sparring partner of mine. After that he laboured to a points win against Larry Donald.

Most of my training took place in Romford. A couple of weeks before the fight, we flew out to Las Vegas to complete our preparation. My team was made up of Freddie King, Mark Allard, Nigel Brightwell, Ian Allcock and my cousin Anthony, while Barry's driver, Robbo, joined us as a minder. He was there to keep an eye on all of us – and on me in particular.

We were staying at the MGM Grand and everything was provided for us there. Whenever we needed to eat something, it was taken care of by the hotel. It was the same if we needed something to drink. It was only when we left the hotel that we needed to pay for anything and, to cover these kinds of expenses, Barry provided us with a generous float.

Robbo was one of the Matchroom family. When I first arrived there he would sometimes take me out in the evenings, after training, to a casino he knew. Gambling was his hobby and he would bet high stakes – a high-roller, as the Americans would say. I was quite happy to go with him because I could eat for free there. Provided Robbo was playing, the food and drinks were on the house. For me that meant I was able to eat a steak every time I went.

I remember seeing Robbo win £100 once, which, to a young fighter who had never had much money of his own, was a huge sum. Robbo wanted to continue playing but I persuaded him that he should quit while he was ahead and leave. It was naïveté on my part, because for somebody like Robbo wins like that were just part of the betting experience. When I mentioned it to Freddie I didn't realise that it would cause trouble, but Freddie hated gambling and word duly filtered back to Barry. In turn, Barry put a stop to our casino visits. At the time I was disappointed about it. I didn't see any harm in it and, besides, I appreciated the free steaks. Now I'm a few years older I can see that Barry did it for the right reasons. He didn't want me, young and impressionable as I was, hanging around a gambling environment. As he saw it, there was a risk that I would develop a liking for it and fritter my money away.

To be good at gambling you sometimes need to be able to spot a winner when very few others can. When Robbo first saw me in Romford he thought I had an aura about me, so much so that he believed I would go on to be the heavyweight champion of the world one day. This was a gut feeling because he had never even seen me fight, but it was still enough for him to tour round the local Ladbrokes shops and bet as much as he could afford. When I beat Michael Bentt in 1994, Robbo collected over £100,000. I'm told that Barry invested it in a house for him before he could start giving it back to the bookies.

We trained at the Top Rank Gym in Las Vegas. Normally there are several boxers who use the place at any one time, but for us they closed it so that we could complete our training without any distractions.

I had been sparring with a local heavyweight called Jonathan Grant. He was 6ft 8in, which meant that he could replicate Riddick's size, but he was also very inexperienced. Riddick was something else entirely. At 6ft 5in he was only 3in taller than I was, but he brought 17st 3lb to the scales at the weigh-in. My weight was 15st 4lb, which meant that Riddick had a weight advantage of 27lb. This was a real heavyweight!

Barry has often said that, if I was naturally 14lb heavier, I would have been one of the all-time greats. I was still essentially a blown-up cruiserweight and a bit of extra weight might have been helpful when I was fighting some of the very big guys. That said, I still think I could have beaten Riddick Bowe if the conditions had been different.

For the first two rounds I controlled the fight. My strategy was to hit and not *get* hit. I was too fast for Riddick, using my jab to open him up and then getting in close to land my combinations. Before he could hit me back I would retreat, not giving him the chance to counter me. He was big, but he was also slow and it felt as if I could run circles around him.

At the end of the first round I smashed my right fist into his jaw. He definitely felt that. You could see that he was becoming disheartened. He thought that I was only a small guy, that I wouldn't be able to cope with his size and strength, but this was the most important fight of my career and I was determined to give it everything I had.

Riddick turned away from me in the second round after our heads clashed. He was complaining about it, looking for help from the referee, Richard Steele. It was a sure sign that he didn't fancy this any more, because it was only a slight knock and not the kind to do any damage. He should have been far more worried about what I was doing to him with my hands, but when things are not going your way little things like this can seem important. I put my hand out to apologise but he ignored it, firing a jab at me instead. When the bell rang he went back to his corner and said to Eddie Futch, his trainer, 'He's too fast. I can't hit him.'

After six minutes all three of the judges had me ahead on their scorecards. They all agreed that I had taken the first two rounds. If I could have continued to box like that, at least for a few more rounds, then the fight would have been mine. Unfortunately, my conditioning wasn't what it needed to be. For the previous fight, against Michael Bentt, I had been fitter than ever before. Jimmy McDonnell had worked wonders with me. Sadly, Jimmy was no longer around and fatigue started to set in.

Freddie was a brilliant trainer. He was tactically very astute and helped me with my combinations, but fitness wasn't his strong point. He would send me out jogging for half an hour when what I needed, as an explosive fighter, was explosive runs. I should have been doing 200 metres and 400 metres, over and over again. This is the way Jimmy had worked with me and the results had been terrific. Before the Bentt fight I had always run into a wall around the fourth round of every fight. That was when fatigue would set in. Against lower-quality opposition it didn't matter because I was good enough to find a way to win, but Riddick Bowe was a world-class heavyweight.

I still think I would have tired eventually against Riddick but, if I had been able to dance around him for a few more rounds, he would also have run out of steam. He would have become even slower, to the point where he would have been throwing one punch at a time. Frustration would have set in and I would have had a golden opportunity to snatch the victory.

As it was, after two rounds of working hard against this huge opponent, I began to slow down. I wasn't able to move the way I wanted to and Riddick dragged me into a brawl, his kind of fight. He knocked me down twice in that third round. I remember looking up at him from the canvas thinking, 'So this is how it feels to get knocked down. This is what I've been doing to people.'

My legs had turned to rubber and I couldn't get out of his way. Again he sent me to the floor twice in the fourth round and then once more in the fifth. He tried to move in for the kill and got careless. He hadn't hurt me as badly as he obviously thought he had and I slammed a right uppercut into his chin. All thoughts of a stoppage victory left his mind for a short time as he grabbed hold of me.

Sadly, it was too little, too late. Riddick caught me again in the sixth, this time with a left hook. I managed to get up again but the barrage of punches that landed as I was trapped against the ropes finished me. Richard Steele counted me out while I was on one knee. I had nothing left.

Seven knockdowns in total. The most in a heavyweight title fight since Tom McNeeley had been floored ten times by Floyd Patterson in 1961. And the Americans loved me for it. They said I was welcome back any time, and that I was one of the bravest fighters they had ever seen.

It may look like that, but bravery doesn't come into it. All I did was what comes naturally to me as a fighter. Riddick Bowe was hitting me, knocking me down, and I was fighting back because that was my instinct. If you talked to me now I would tell you that I should have stayed down rather than repeatedly get back up on my feet. What was the point in taking all of that punishment in a fight I was losing anyway? Nobody paid me extra for taking a beating, so what did I have to gain? The answer is, in the ring you follow your instincts and not your common sense. It was about two men, Herbie Hide and Riddick Bowe, and as long as I hadn't been counted out I was still in the fight.

While I didn't feel brave, I wasn't afraid either. Those blows weren't hurting me but they were making me feel dazed. He was just big but he wasn't better.

Sometimes you lose. As a professional boxer you have to accept that, particularly if you are prepared to face the toughest fighters out there. There was no shame in it and I didn't blame anybody. I just felt disappointed for the people who had come to support me, and even more so for Alan, who was in terrible pain with his illness but still made it all the way to Las Vegas to cheer me on.

Riddick said later that he had never been hit so hard by any other fighter, and he's been in with quite a few top-class heavyweights, so there is, at least, a moral victory for me there.

The money I made from the fight was important, but it was scant consolation for the loss of my belt. Ask any champion which they would prefer, a penny to win or a million to lose, and the answer will always be the same. It's just the nature of the beast.

Chapter 8

Building Bawburgh

When I was living in the house at Brentwood, my housemates would be spending all their cash on clothes and going out. I would wear whichever clothes I had in my wardrobe and I didn't worry too much about impressing other people. It wasn't that I was tight. I was just good with my finances. I wasn't earning much money, so I cut my cloth accordingly. Then I bought myself a pair of moccasins, proudly telling the others that they had set me back £80.

Errol looked at them and scratched his head. 'You know what, Herbie?' he said. 'I don't think your shoes cost you as much as that.'

'Why do you say that?' I was lying on the coach in the living room with my feet resting on the upholstery.

'They don't look like £80 shoes, that's all.'

'What do £80 shoes look like then?'

'Like those, but without the sticker saying £7.99 on the sole.'

Nothing But Trouble

That was me to a tee. The others might have laughed, but I was just living within my means.

All of that penny pinching changed after the Riddick Bowe fight. Overnight I had become a millionaire and at only 22 I had more money than I could possibly spend. Of course, there were one or two things I wanted to spend my newfound riches on, starting with a house.

Barry had always helped me to take care of my finances. Long before he became a sports promoter he had studied to become a chartered accountant, so he knew how to look after his affairs. He used this knowledge to enable me to make the best of the money I had earned against Riddick Bowe. The $3.1 million was worth roughly £2 million then and, because I also held Nigerian citizenship, Barry felt that it was best for me to put the money into an offshore trust. That way I wouldn't be stung too heavily by the taxman. He advised my accountant regarding the formalities and helped us to get clearance with the Inland Revenue. This meant that the house I wanted to build would, at least in principle, belong to the trust because I was going to pay for it with some of the funds from the Bowe fight.

The plot of farmland I bought was in Bawburgh, a few miles from the centre of Norwich and, once a few ramshackle old barns had been flattened, I started building the house. Having a place that I could call my own was important to me and I wanted something that was fit for a world heavyweight champion, or a former heavyweight champion, as I then was.

Actually, before the first bricks could be laid we had great fun shooting rabbits on the land. It was Nigel

Building Bawburgh

Brightwell's idea. He thought it would be a good laugh and all he needed to do was convince Mark Allard, who had the rifles and the licence to use them, that it would be worthwhile.

Mark is one of my oldest friends from Norwich. He used to fight as an amateur at the Lads' Club and after I joined he would take me under his wing, even dragging me along to nightclubs when I was only 14 or 15. But that wasn't all he did for me. Many was the time that he would pick me up in his car and take me to a local fight or for something to eat at his mum's house.

He had been at the Lads' Club for a long time, but I think he was probably too nervous to make it as a boxer. When we sparred, which for me was like trying to punch a fly, he would compliment me the whole while, saying things like, 'Good punch, Herbie!' and, 'That's the way!' Maybe he thought I would go easy on him if he flattered me like that.

One thing I didn't realise, even as a heavyweight champion, was that Mark believed I was crazy. He didn't want to come hunting with us because he wasn't sure what I would do when I had a rifle in my hands.

There are those who feel that by building a mansion I was just showing off, demonstrating how wealthy I was, but that wasn't the case at all. I built that house because it was what I wanted, for myself and not for onlookers. There's an old saying that says you have to earn respect, but you get envy for free. With that in mind, I sincerely believe that you can try to suit only yourself, because there will always be people who want to point the finger and criticise you. The house gave me the confidence I needed to feel like a man who had achieved something.

Nothing But Trouble

Nobody could take away the glory of my first world title, but this house was made of bricks and mortar and it was a foundation for my future.

With Norwich being Norwich, there was a great deal of local media attention focused on the building site. Pictures were printed depicting various stages of the construction process, and reports surfaced describing the eight bedrooms, snooker room, swimming pool and disco. The total price of £1 million that the press estimated for the building work was reasonably accurate, although that went up once I requested improvements to the original plans.

People talk in Norwich and I heard some stories that were quite incredible. I was visiting a club in Norwich with Helen while the house was being built, and a young lady approached me and said, 'A friend of mine was at a party at your house recently. She told me all about it. She says that you were all in the pool and it was lovely.'

I don't know what she was talking about because the house wasn't ready to live in, never mind to make use of the pool. 'Yes,' I told her. 'The pool's superb. It'll be even more amazing once it's been tiled so that we can fill it with water.'

That kind of thing was just a result of the media attention. However, I have to say that, even though there is a disco built into the house, it's not like a town-centre nightclub. It's more of a party room that we use occasionally when somebody has a birthday or there's an after-fight get-together. I am careful about who I invite to the house because you can never be sure what they will start telling people afterwards, so there are only a select few people who would have been inside it. The fact is, when I am at home I am very quiet and don't like having guests all the time.

In America it's quite normal for big houses to incorporate a degree of entertainment into their design, and that was what I wanted to create at Bawburgh. It is somewhere my family can live and my friends can visit, and everybody can relax there and enjoy themselves.

Once the building work was underway, I was able to focus on my other weakness – cars. Ask any young man of that age what he would spend his money on and most of them would say the same. I didn't have to dream about them: I was in a position where I could buy them for cash. At one point I had so many motors sitting around my home that they wouldn't fit in the garages. The house at Bawburgh has three garages, meaning that some of them would be parked on the forecourt. It got to the stage where I had a Bentley, a Porsche convertible, an Audi convertible and a Mercedes S Series all parked up and doing nothing. I would use my Range Rover only for my day-to-day activities, leaving all the other cars virtually unused. My secretary once told me that I had a house parked in my garage. By this she meant that the value of each car was enough to buy an ordinary house.

It never really occurred to me how daft I must have appeared to other people until a gentleman who came to the house once a month to train my Rottweilers mentioned that the Bentley hadn't moved an inch since his last visit. He was genuinely shocked that I could have car like that and not use it. That's when it dawned on me how embarrassing it was to have all these vehicles sitting around the place. It wasn't as if I was getting any enjoyment from them. All I was doing was showing off my purchasing power.

The dogs were another hobby of mine. I had various breeds but my favourites were the Rottweilers. As they bred I would keep the puppies, instead of moving them on, and at one point I must have had 25 dogs at the house.

I also made sure that my dogs had a good pedigree. I bought one that had been intended for the Sultan of Brunei. He cost me £2,500.

These weren't pets: they were working dogs and they were trained to kill. Although this guy came to train them, I would also teach them myself. They were vicious creatures, more dangerous than police dogs and, if somebody had been foolish enough to break into my property, the Rottweilers would literally have ripped them to shreds.

A journalist from *Boxing News* once visited me at home and wanted to take a photo of one of my dogs, Chico. He was attached to a chain at a safe distance, so nothing could happen, and I said to Chico, 'Kill!' He jumped at the guy and would have torn his throat out if he had been able to get close enough. Needless to say, the resulting picture was fantastic.

The dogs were good for company, but also for protection. This sounds strange coming from somebody who beats people up for a living and is supposed to be fearless, but I don't like being by myself. In fact, I have never spent a night alone at my house in Bawburgh. People have never frightened me but I am terrified of ghosts. Even though I know it's daft for a man in his late 30s to think about such things, I still sleep with the light on.

Building Bawburgh

The only time I can remember being left on my own in Brentwood, when we had been to see Jimmy McDonnell fight against Kenny Vice at the Royal Albert Hall, I brought my mattress downstairs into the living room and slept by the television. Ian Allcock was with me at the fight and went to the hospital with Jimmy afterwards, while I went home by myself. He came back to the house later and almost fell over me when he walked in.

As I was building the house at Bawburgh, I rented a place in Norwich where I could live while the property was being completed. At a guess I would say that the house was about 50 years old, and I had no idea what had gone on there in the past. I even asked my Auntie Winnie, who worked for British Telecom and was able to check up on these sorts of things, to find out who had lived there before me. She told me that a young couple had had the place, but she probably said that just to put me at ease. Looking at the curtains, which were probably first used in the Old Testament period, I was sure that old people had been living there. What concerned me was that these old people may well have died in the house, leaving their ghosts inside the place.

I will live only in a newly built house, or one whose history I can be sure of. The older the house, the greater the chance that somebody is haunting it. Moving into a stately home would never be an option for me.

Neil Featherby was one of the worst for winding me up with tales of haunted houses and spooks. He told me that the ghost of a headless horseman roamed the area at night, and that when the horse wasn't being used it would be chained up in the nearby meadow. I was always stupid enough to listen to his stories, even though I knew

Nothing But Trouble

I shouldn't, and by the time he left me I would be petrified. It was the same with horror films on television: I would watch them even though I knew I wouldn't be able to sleep afterwards.

A lot of this is rooted in my childhood. Back in Nigeria I would fight with the other children who lived nearby. There was an old man called Humphrey who disliked me because I would beat his grandchildren up. They were older than I was, but that didn't matter because I was bigger. To Humphrey, a big man himself with a reputation locally as a leader, it highlighted a weakness in his family and he hated me for it.

One night when I was sleeping I dreamt that Humphrey was calling to me. His arm was outstretched, beckoning me towards him. I remember his old grey beard and his yellow teeth, but there was something dangerous in his eyes that made him seem more frightening than ever before. The more he called to me, the more afraid I became and I refused to go to him.

I woke up, sweating and shivering at the same time. My grandmother saw me and just held me, asking what I had seen.

Then we heard a commotion coming from one of the other huts. It was Humphrey's wife. She was screaming because Humphrey had just died. He must have been passing away while I was dreaming about him.

In my part of Nigeria we have a belief that old people take a young soul with them when they die. Years ago a small child would be sacrificed when one of the elders died. These days they will kill a dog instead. My feeling is that Humphrey was trying to take me as his sacrifice by entering my sleep and calling me to him. It's only because I was strong enough to refuse him, and was able to wake up, that he went alone.

He was an evil man, one who was willing to end the life of a young boy, and because of him I am unable to trust anything, or anybody, that I cannot see or feel. Spirits are all around us and not all of them are good.

The time arrived when I needed to make a return to the ring, not for monetary reasons (although I did want to keep the cash flowing) but because fighting is what I do. The break did me good, but the house and my collection of cars weren't enough to keep me happy. I had kept myself fit in the year I had been away from the ring, so getting back to the rigours of training wasn't going to be an issue. During that period there had been talk of a challenge for the European championship against Îeljko Mavroviç in Germany, but I turned that down because I wanted to concentrate on completing the house before I fought again. The greater problem was that I now had to decide which direction my career should take. My contract with Barry had run out and new offers needed to be considered.

Frank Warren was attracting a lot of the UK's major boxers to his Sports Network outfit at the time, so I chose to join him. He also had a contract with BSkyB, which meant that his boxers would be fighting regularly and getting well paid. This is something that Barry was unable to offer me, at least not on the same scale.

Leaving Barry wasn't something I really wanted to do. He had always been very fair to me and we got along very well with each other. I had also earned more by fighting for him than I would have by fighting for

Warren. Perhaps if I had been a few years older, I might have realised how good things were for me at Matchroom, but I was young and easily influenced by other people.

I first began to have my doubts about Barry – unfounded ones – when I was training for the Michael Bentt fight. Jimmy McDonnell told me to be wary of him. He felt very bitter about the way he was paid for his fight with Azumah Nelson in November 1989. I was making my second professional appearance on the undercard that evening, so I was much too green to know the ins and outs of boxing politics. It was Jimmy's second crack at a world title and he was looking for a bumper payday. For his loss against Brian Mitchell – his first championship fight, which had taken place a year earlier – he told me that he had earned £15,000. That was a Mickey Duff promotion, so Barry had nothing to do with it, though he did make it clear that Jimmy should expect a much better deal this time around. The press had asked him what Jimmy would earn and he told them that he would add at least a nought to the figure, though his payment was more to the tune of £50,000. I had a different kind of agreement with Barry. He would pay me in advance of every fight via a non-returnable bank transfer, so it was always what I expected it to be. But the main reason for my move to Sports Network was my relationship with John Hornewer. He had been advising me on various matters and he felt that it might be a worthwhile move.

John and I first met in 1990 when he had been working with Frank Maloney and Lennox Lewis, and I had been a very young pro. He was in England to see Lennox fight

Noel Quarless at the York Hall in a show that Barry was promoting, and I had been invited along to sit in the audience. We got talking afterwards and I asked him why a boxer would need a lawyer. That's how naïve I was in those days. In any case, I wasn't making any money yet, so all of this was a bit foreign to me.

That was the last I saw of him for four years. Then, in Atlantic City when Lennox defended his WBC title against Phil Jackson, we met again. We chatted for a while and he agreed to work with me. He was instrumental in making sure that I was paid correctly for the fight with Riddick Bowe, ensuring that my purse from the HBO network would be forthcoming by organising a letter of credit. A lot of people had an input into that fight, but I will always be thankful to John for his help.

After Bowe had beaten me and I took a long time out, John and I would talk often. He was somebody I had grown to trust and respect, and his opinion counted for a lot with me. He believed that Warren would give me a couple of fights to shake off the rust and then unleash me on the better fighters, rather than pitch me straight into a championship fight, where I might be exposed. Barry always had my best interests at heart, but so did John, and I chose to listen to him.

I wasn't the first fighter to leave Matchroom for Sports Network. Prince Naseem Hamed, Chris Eubank, Scott Welsh and Steve Collins all did the same. Once, when I met up with Robbo in London after I had joined Warren, I asked him, 'How's Barry?'

'He got a sore arse,' he told me.

'Why's that then?'

Nothing But Trouble

'All his boxers have fucked him. You fucked him and left, Eubank fucked him, Naseem fucked him and so did Steve Collins.'

That said it all, really. Not that Barry would have thought about it in those crude terms. Warren was able to provide something that Barry couldn't. To Barry it was just business and people would follow the best offer. People had left Warren before to fight for Barry, so he was philosophical about it.

I'm not going to pretend that I like Frank Warren. I don't. You can read a lot into somebody by the strength of their handshake, and with Warren there was absolutely no power there. Taking his flaccid hand felt like grabbing one of those rubber chickens you find in joke shops. For all that, Warren had risen from organising unlicensed boxing shows in London to being one of the world's leading promoters. He's a man who has had more ups and downs in his career than even I have.

There was a shooting that very nearly cost him his life in 1989, when a masked gunman opened fire with a Luger pistol. The bullet narrowly missed his heart. Terry Marsh, the former IBF light-welterweight champion was charged with attempted murder but was acquitted at the subsequent trial.

That attempt on his life led him to the brink of bankruptcy but his instincts as a businessman enabled him to regroup. It took a while, but when I joined him he had worked his way back up to the top of the sport. Warren had everything to offer: the deal with BSkyB, big-hall boxing shows and the contacts to get me another world-title shot in the shortest space of time. It made perfect business sense to join forces with him, despite any reservations I had.

We agreed that my return to the ring would be on the undercard of the first fight between Nigel Benn and Steve Collins, the first boxing event to be staged at the new Nynex Arena in Manchester, against my old adversary Michael Murray.

The move to Warren meant that I would have to leave Freddie King. Freddie was Barry's man, a loyal partner, and there was no way that I could continue working with him if I wasn't on Barry's payroll. He was a hard act to follow and I wanted to make sure that, whoever I chose, it would be somebody who could work on that level. That's why I decided to move to Brendan Ingle's Wincobank gym in Sheffield.

Brendan was a man I admired immensely. Most people think of Naseem Hamed when Wincobank is mentioned. Some would say that Naseem was already a natural talent and that anybody could have taken him to championship level, but I don't agree. It was Brendan who moulded him into the fighter he became, and Brendan who instilled the razzmatazz for which Naz was so well known. But I was more impressed with his work with other fighters, guys who had the tools but needed help on a psychological level to be successful in the ring. Brendan was the kind of trainer who would make you believe that you were the best fighter on the planet, that anything was possible and that you just needed to go out and take it. Just look at somebody like Johnny Nelson. He was just a journeyman with low self-esteem before he teamed up with Brendan, but Brendan turned him into a world champion.

Brendan also had a particular way in which he liked his boxers to fight. His boys were attack minded and fought with flair. Wincobank fighters were fun to watch, just like me. It seemed like the perfect move.

While I was still a young fighter at Matchroom I was invited to Wincobank to spar with Johnny Nelson, so I already knew Brendan. Back then he had helped me to overcome my stammer. He had organised digs for me to stay in while I was there and then invited the owners of the house over to the gym.

'Meet the people you'll be staying with,' he said. I introduced myself, stuttering away as I did it.

Then their 18-year-old followed them into the room. When I started talking to her the stammer disappeared.

'Come here, you African, womanising bastard,' he said, grabbing me by the ear. 'Why didn't you stammer when you were talking to that young girl?'

'B-b-b-because . . .'

'Because you are such a womaniser and you know how to stop your stammer,' he told me.

He was right too. Subconsciously I was able to control it when I needed to, as Brendan had suspected all along.

Training with Brendan was a little different from what I had previously experienced. His boys were taught to block the punches, something I wasn't used to. Some of his training methods were also a bit unorthodox.

While I was there he took us to a local Category B prison to meet the inmates. Some of South Yorkshire's finest were locked up in there and we were asked to spar with a few of them in a makeshift gym Brendan had set up in the sports hall. At a guess I would say we had about 500 prisoners watching us that day, and

Brendan, with all his Irish charm and natural charisma, had them in the palm of his hand. For those guys it was wonderful entertainment.

Certain inmates, those who felt brave enough, were invited into the ring so that they could try to hit us. There were a few of us from the gym there, including Ryan Rhodes and Johnny Nelson, and the rules were that the prisoners were allowed to hit us, or at least attempt to, but we were not to hit them back. I already knew this when my turn to fight came, stepping up to face a lifer who looked intent on taking my head off. He rushed forward towards me, swinging wildly and missing with most of his punches but catching me with one or two, and I reverted to my instincts. A beautifully delivered left hook to his ribs saw him collapse like a bag of sand. All the Wincobank fighters had been goading me, telling me to 'take no prisoners', but they shut up when that happened.

'What are you trying to do, get us all killed?' Brendan screamed at me. He was over like a shot to make sure I didn't hit this guy again. With 500 of his fellow inmates crowding the hall, I don't think Brendan fancied his chances of getting out of there in one piece. It wasn't a big deal though. The guy got up and completed the round with me.

Some believe that I felt uncomfortable at Wincobank. It's true that I was used to being one of the biggest names in the gym, but it wasn't important to me. As long as I get paid I don't mind who is training alongside me. Naseem – already a world champion when I arrived in Sheffield, and on the verge of becoming an international star – was the star of the show in the gym. The media attention was focused on him more than anybody else, but that didn't bother me at all. I needed to rebuild my career after the loss to Bowe, so I didn't expect the world to revolve around me. In any case, when I was moving up the ranks at Matchroom I had been training alongside some other big names, so this kind of thing was nothing new to me.

I also got on very well with many of the boxers there. I think Jonathan Thaxton, a former Lads' Club boxer, had mentioned that I wasn't very popular with certain people in Norwich, but the Sheffield boys made it very clear that they were very happy to have me on board. Jonathan and I both came from Norwich, but that was about all we had in common. Jonathan is a local Norfolk lad, quiet and well mannered, who has been very successful at domestic level. That's not always enough to get the fans interested, and he can be thankful that I was there at the same time to garner some interest in the Norfolk boxing scene.

Jonathan benefited because I was making headlines and, let's face it, anybody is going to look like an angel next to me. I was always in the papers for one thing or another, rubbing my success and wealth in people's faces. Maybe that's why certain people in Norfolk who objected to me took Jonathan to heart. He was one of them; the way he acted, the way he spoke, the way he didn't build a huge mansion right under their noses. The only problem for him was that he would be earning less for his fights than I would be receiving in expenses for mine. Some of his best purses were earned from appearing on the undercard of my shows.

We don't know each other very well, even though we both come from the same city. He's not really the kind of guy I would hang around with privately. With somebody like Jackson Williams, another naïve local boy who boxes out of Norwich, I would do anything. He's an angel and I would expect him to turn a blind eye to my bad-boy exploits.

The fight against Murray was a letdown. I had beaten him before and there was never any danger that he would beat me this time around. He was just a body as far as I was concerned, a stepping stone to more meaningful contests. As I remember it, the arena was virtually empty. It was a couple of hours before the main bout and most of the crowd hadn't yet arrived – a far cry from that night at the MGM Grand in Las Vegas.

When we had met the first time, his strategy had been to stay away from me and try not to get hurt. It wasn't much different in this fight. I staggered him with a left hook and, before I could follow up with my right hand, he took a knee. What the hell! I let him have the right anyway. It was frustration on my part and the referee was straight over to reprimand me. Brendan was up on the apron like a shot, hollering at the referee that it was no foul, that Murray wasn't yet on one knee by the time I landed that right. Brendan is a wily old pro and was well aware of how nervous the referees can be on big shows like this, especially when it is clear that a huge investment has been made in one of the fighters and not the other.

I am well known for hitting people while they are on the way down. Once I sense that somebody is hurt I just want to get the job completed as quickly as possible, and it was the same with Michael Murray. My punches were landing and I could sense victory, and then he went and took a knee to destroy my momentum. There's a lovely feeling about inflicting pain upon your opponent and knocking him out cleanly, and that was all I was looking for when I landed the late punch.

In the sixth round I stopped Murray but it was hard work. My condition had been terrible. I hadn't had a fight for 16 months and after throwing the first punch I felt exhausted. It was a relief to get the contest over and done with.

Steve beat Nigel in the main event that night, but nobody was really satisfied because Nigel had been forced to pull out after injuring his ankle. The inevitable rematch was duly organised for November 1996 and I was again asked to fight on the undercard in Manchester. Little Frankie Swindell was my opponent and I knocked him out in the first round. He was only 5ft 10in and looked more like a light-heavyweight. Even so, he brought 225lb to the scales so he was half a stone heavier than I was.

He's one of those guys who have fought, and lost to, just about everybody on the heavyweight scene. He had two cracks at the light-heavyweight title earlier in his career, but by the time I faced him he was being served up as another victim. He had already been in with other world champions, such as Henry Akinwande, Michael Moorer and Tony Tucker. After facing me he went in with Chris Byrd and Hasim Rahman. Maybe he was nothing more than an opponent, but none of those boxers ever put him away in the first round, as I did.

For the first time in my life I felt afraid going into that fight. A feeling of nervousness and uncertainty hit me when we arrived in Manchester, shortly before the event. My main concern was about Graham Everett, who had

Even in my school days I was larger than life, as this picture of the school cricket team shows.

Left: Butter wouldn't melt... Who would have guessed that this shy young boy with a stammer would go on to be champion of the world?

My amateur career was brief, but successful nonetheless.

Only our mothers can tell us apart – since the early days at Matchroom I have shared a great friendship with Francis Ampofo.

Chilling out at my mum and dad's house in Eaton.

My younger brother Alan was my biggest fan before he lost his brave fight with leukaemia in 1997. Here he is enjoying his friend Robin's company.

I beat Conroy Nelson to win my first title – the WBC International heavyweight championship. Freddie King (*left*) and Alex Gower hoisted me aloft as the crowd in Norwich Sports Village went wild.

arry Hearn, a great man and the best promoter I ever worked with was one of the first to ongratulate me after the Nelson fight.

Above: My win over Michael Murray in Dagenham brought me the British Heavyweight title, but I cried all the way home after my performance was heavily criticised.

Below: Things turned nasty at the press conference to announce my challenge to Michael Bentt for his WBO title at The New Den. Here we are brawling after I knocked his hat off.

now taken over as my head trainer from Brendan Ingle. For my whole career I had been looked after by experienced coaches. Suddenly I was going into the ring without Freddie King or Brendan beside me, and it frightened me. Did Graham have the know-how to take charge of my corner? Would he know what to do if I got into trouble? These were the questions that were bothering me, and it was only after Nigel Brightwell, my old mate from the Lads' Club, talked me round that I felt confident enough to go through with it. Nigel had always been very supportive and was very good at motivating me.

'You know what your problem is?' he asked me when I told him how I was feeling. 'You've spent so long playing about with your house that you've forgotten you're a boxer.'

'What about Michael Murray then? I didn't feel scared before that fight, did I?'

'No, because you'd already fought him once and you knew that you had nothing to be afraid of. This time it's different. You've been spending your life in nightclubs and at the house, and now you have to get back to fighting, and that's what's so frightening.'

He was right. It was all in my head. I just had to overcome my own anxieties and then I would have no problem beating Frankie Swindell. If it hadn't been for Nigel, there would have been no fight. Who knows if I would have had a career left after that? Boxing is a hurting business and a fighter needs to be in the right frame of mind. Thanks to Nigel I was able to control my fears and, after that, I never worried like that again.

Chapter 9

The Two-Time Champion

I think Tony Tucker enjoyed his trip to Norwich to fight me for the vacant WBO title. It's certainly a long way removed from the glitz and glamour of Las Vegas, the location of his four other world-title fights. We met on the evening of 28 June 1997, a date that will for ever be remembered in boxing circles for one of the most shameful events in the history of the sport after Mike Tyson bit a chunk out of Evander Holyfield's ear in their fight at the MGM Grand in Las Vegas. It was also one of the greatest nights of my career.

The fight fell into my lap faster than I had anticipated. At the time I was convinced that I still had the tools to become heavyweight champion again, but I was also realistic enough to believe that I needed a few more bouts under my belt before one of the sanctioning bodies would look at me as a plausible challenger.

Frank Warren had called to offer me a shot at the British title and I was happy with that. As well as providing me with a useful step-up on the ladder towards more meaningful fights, it also meant that I would be able to do something for Alan, who by now was entering the final stages of his battle against leukaemia. His time with us was running out quickly and I wanted to do one last thing to make him proud. I figured that, if I won the British title, I could give him the belt as a present.

We were in the car together when I mentioned it to Alan. 'I have some good news. They're going to let me fight for the British title,' I told him.

His reaction surprised me. I expected him to be delighted, but he just kept quiet.

'Alan, did you hear what I just said to you?' I asked him. 'I'm going to get the British heavyweight belt and give it to you.'

'Why the British title?' he asked. 'I want a world title.'

I would have done anything for him at this stage, but I couldn't see how I could get him a world championship so quickly. 'Alan,' I reasoned with him, 'I've got to get a title challenge first. I have to win this.'

It made no difference. Only a world championship belt would make him happy.

Then, later that day as I arrived home, there was another call from Warren. He had been talking with Don King about the vacant WBO title. When I contacted him he offered me the fight against Tony Tucker. It was as if God had wanted it that way.

Tony was one of the so-called 'forgotten generation' of heavyweights, a group of fighters who managed to win and lose the championship during the 1980s with alarming regularity. It was an era often unfavourably compared to the decade that preceded it, when legends such as Muhammad Ali, Joe Frazier and George Foreman graced the sport. As those names eventually grew older and faded from view, the division was left with a dearth of talent. Larry Holmes was the only fighter who deserved to call himself the champ, but he concentrated on a version of the belt belonging to the newly formed International Boxing Federation. Although the WBO belt had not yet been introduced, two other versions of the title were still available and the remaining rabble fought it out among themselves.

It's fair to say that when Tony beat James 'Buster' Douglas to claim the vacant IBF championship in 1986, he wasn't the greatest ever heavyweight champion. But he was a better fighter than many of the title holders of that period. He took Mike Tyson – the real Mike Tyson, as opposed to the empty shell of a fighter who later lost to Danny Williams – the full 12 rounds when they met. This was Tony's first defence of the championship and, although he lost on points, he did manage to rattle Mike in the first round.

He gave Lennox Lewis a run for his money too. Lennox won comfortably on points when they met in 1993 but, in the closing rounds, it was Tony who was the more aggressive fighter. By the time we met, Tony had experienced some hard times. Even so, he continued to fight at a high level and, after his fights against Tyson and Lewis, he had made other quality heavyweights, such as Bruce Seldon and Henry Akinwande, work hard for their money. After meeting me he extended John Ruiz, the future three-time world champion, into the 11th round before being stopped. Apart from me, he proved a handful for every other fighter he faced.

Nothing But Trouble

For my previous world-championship fights Freddie King had been in my corner. While it wasn't possible for me to work with Freddie for this fight, Frank still felt that I needed to have somebody he trusted as my trainer. He wanted me to work with Jimmy McDonnell. As I have already said, Jimmy and I go back a long way. When I first arrived at Matchroom Jimmy was the top man there and I looked up to him. He was at the peak of his career, having beaten Barry McGuigan. Young boxers need somebody like that to set an example, to help them motivate themselves. Sadly, Jimmy never won another fight after that. He was granted the title shot against the great Azumah Nelson for the WBC super-featherweight title the following November but he was knocked down four times before being stopped in the final round. His career as a boxer went downhill after that, but he remained with Matchroom as a fitness trainer. He joined up with Frank Warren and, since then, he has become quite successful as a trainer.

We did most of our training for the Tucker fight at Jim's gym in London. At this time I still had a flat in Chadwell Heath near Romford, but it was easier for me to stay in a hotel in north London so that I would be near to the gym.

One evening after training I met up with some friends at a restaurant in Tottenham for some African food and a bottle of Guinness. It was a particularly stressful period for me because, as well as my training for a hugely important fight and needing to give a hundred per cent in the gym every day, Alan's condition was worsening. He was in and out of hospital over in Norwich and I was on the telephone to my parents at every opportunity to check up on him. Going out gave me a chance to unwind, to let off some steam.

Furthermore, I had just forked out £150,000 for a new Bentley and I was keen to show it off. This was just another in a long line of fancy cars. For some people it's an ambition to drive a car like this. For me it was a case of proving to myself that I could have anything I wanted. Getting the car was the important part. After that it was just another car as far as I was concerned.

After the meal I left my friends and drove back towards the hotel by myself. I saw a pretty girl standing at the side of the road so I pulled over, thinking that she would be impressed by the Bentley. We got talking and then she suggested that we have sex. Perhaps I was being incredibly naïve because, even at this point, it hadn't occurred to me that she was just touting for business. She wanted to know if we could do it in the car.

From out of nowhere a car pulled up behind us and two men stepped out. 'Can you move away, please,' the first man told me.

'Are you for real?' I asked him. 'You can see me chatting to a pretty girl and you ask me if I can move away?'

'We are police officers,' he said.

'So what? I'm talking to a pretty girl so why have I got to move out of the way?'

'This young lady is a prostitute,' he told me, 'and we have reason to believe that you are soliciting for sex.'

'Do you think I'm trying to fuck her? Well, even if I am, I'm not planning on paying for it.' That was the truth. I was unfamiliar with this part of London and I hadn't known that this was a red-light district. In any case, I had very little cash on me, having spent my money in the African restaurant, and to prove this I asked them to search me. They refused and arrested me for kerb crawling.

By the time I finally arrived back at the hotel I was in a foul mood. This was really the last thing I needed – kerb crawling is embarrassing enough under any circumstances, but the fact that I had been driving the Bentley just made matters worse.

The following evening I had been due to attend a boxing dinner with Jimmy but I called him up in the morning to explain what had happened and that I needed some time for myself. He listened to what I had to say and told me that he understood. He went to the dinner by himself while I travelled back home to Norwich.

The dinner was attended by several members of the press and, while I had hoped to keep this little matter quiet, word still got out. After that, it was all over the national newspapers: HERBIE HIDE CAUGHT KERB CRAWLING IN NEW BENTLEY. I became a laughing stock – even Frank Warren thought it was funny.

After just one more fight I decided that Jimmy and I had to go our separate ways. Perhaps I was too young to realise what he was trying to do for me at that time, but later it dawned on me that Freddie King had been the kind of trainer a boxer could really rely on. I was often too stubborn and suspicious to allow him to get as close to me as he would have liked at the time. While our relationship was never as strong as it might have been, I was determined that I would have a strong bond with my future trainers. But although I was going to move on from Jimmy, right at that point, with a world title bout only weeks away and with my pre-fight preparation at an advanced stage, it would have been crazy to change my trainer.

Jimmy was a funny guy. Just being around him would make me crease up, although I don't think that he really meant to make me laugh. There was just something about him. He's only a small guy. With his cockney accent he sounds like someone from *Grange Hill*. It was also good fun to wind him up, like the time he overheard a conversation between me and Scott Welsh about Frank Warren. Jimmy was loyal to Warren and began taking his side. Scott looked at him in mock shock and said, 'Jimmy, look at your tongue.'

'What is it?' asked Jimmy, looking suddenly very concerned.

'It's completely brown,' he told him. 'I think it must have been stuck to Warren's arse.'

Jimmy was looking after both Scott Welsh and me at this time. Scott, whom I also knew well from my days at Matchroom, was due to fight on the undercard in Norwich, so we spent a lot of time training together. Usually, I got along very well with him but we would often bicker at each other. We were both heavyweights but I was the one who had enjoyed more success.

After winning his rematch with the late James Oyebola in 1995 he waited a few weeks and then, when we were in the car together one day, asked me why I had not been to his dressing room to congratulate him.

'Scott,' I told him, 'I didn't need to call you, because you won. You didn't need me there, because you had a lot of hangers-on to do that for you, kissing your arse. When you need me is after you lose. That's when your hangers-on will run away and your true friends will stand by you.'

Nothing But Trouble

It was true. I only had to think back to his first fight with Oyebola. That night James had knocked him out in the fifth round of their fight in Atlantic City and I was the only person who had been there for him. Even his trainer had gone. Scott was in a bad way and I was the one who helped him back to his dressing room. Once there I even helped him to remove his shoes. That, to me, was a sign of genuine friendship. I was there for him when nobody else was.

One morning, during training for the Tucker fight, Scott, Jimmy and I were out on the running track. I can't really remember what we were arguing about – it was usually something pretty trivial – but this time it escalated to the point where I squared up to him. Jimmy, who had boxed as a super-featherweight, tried to get in between us to break it up. I'm not sure what he hoped to achieve against two heavyweights but it worked, if only because the sight of him standing there with his little arms stretched out was so funny. He made us go back to the gym before we could start going at each other again – Jimmy wanted me to take out my aggression on Tony Tucker instead.

There were people in the media who believed that I would struggle against Tony. Their logic was that I was too small. My fight against Riddick Bowe had demonstrated that a good big guy will beat a good little guy, but you could not apply the same rule to my fight with Tony. For one thing, Riddick was in his prime when we met in Las Vegas. He was probably the best heavyweight in the world at that time. Tony, on the other hand, was 38 years old and several years past his best form. Even when Tony was at his most dangerous, around the time he fought Tyson in 1987, I don't believe that a prime Riddick Bowe would have had too many difficulties with him. The comparisons were based on size alone, and it was nonsense to believe that I would face the same problems against Tony that I had encountered against Riddick. That said, Tony was still a dangerous proposition. He demonstrated how much he had left when he almost beat John Ruiz a few months after we met.

Warren believed that Tony would probably last 12 rounds with me. For this reason he was happy to be able to schedule the fight for the same day as the Holyfield vs Tyson fight. It meant that Don King, Tony's promoter, would be in Las Vegas and not in Norwich. In his place he sent his stepson, Carl King.

Tony was in Norwich for quite a long time. He spent about a month there in total, training for the fight and making friends with the locals. He found God and his faith played an important role in his life. He would go to church every day. While I was away in London, concentrating fully on what I considered to be the most important fight of my life, Tony was making me look aloof by visiting schools and talking to the kids. People in Norwich were starting to warm to him. Alan would sometimes call me at the training camp and describe how Tony had been on television again. The cameras seemed to be rolling wherever he appeared. Forget about Herbie Hide, Tony Tucker might as well have been the local boy.

There was a time when I would do this kind of thing, visiting schools and opening fêtes. Les King would talk me around Norfolk, getting my face in the papers and gathering positive publicity, but after a while I got bored with the whole scenario. I felt that people were taking us for granted and that they often didn't really appreciate the time and effort that went into these visits. Perhaps for this reason I did now seem aloof, or even arrogant, to the people of Norwich. It had come to the stage where anybody who faced me would be looked upon favourably, and Tony was making all the right moves. He was becoming an angel in the eyes of some Norwich folk.

At the weigh-in in Norwich his reception was far better than mine. I was booed as I stepped up to the scales. As I say, I had been away from Norwich in the time leading up to the fight and it was only now that I sensed that public opinion had turned against me for this fight, but that was to change. Tony did a great job of charming the Norwich people right up until his walk-in in Norwich Sports Village. I entered the ring first and plenty of people were calling for my head. He was then accompanied to the ring, with his American flags flying aloft, by the United States Air Force and it was at this point that the 7,000 people in attendance began to see that this guy was not one of them after all. His cheers turned to boos. The people knew now that Herbie Hide was representing Norwich.

As I saw it, Tony was standing between me and my dream of bringing the belt home for Alan. It wasn't anything personal, he was just in the wrong place at the wrong time. Once the bell rang I went straight at him and traded punches with him in the middle of the ring. He had never taken a beating like this before, nor would he do so again. I was so powerful, so fast, and every punch I threw was finding him. I put him down three times in the second round, catching him with left hooks for the first two knockdowns before I let the bombs fly and he went down a third time. The WBO stipulated that three knockdowns in a round meant that the fight would be automatically stopped. I was world champion for the second time and I had taken less than six minutes to complete the job. Not even Tyson had managed that. The crowd had turned full circle and were now chanting my name: 'Herbie! Herbie!'

Warren had been talking about bringing Tyson over to England. A fight between the pair of us, outdoors at Norwich City's ground, Carrow Road, would have been massive and I believe I could have beaten him. Holyfield made his life hell in their first fight and he wasn't as good as I was. It's a shame that Tyson had to spoil it by getting himself banned from the sport a few hours later.

Sometimes it can be strange how you meet people again later in life under completely different circumstances. I saw Tony again when I was training in Las Vegas in 2006 and he was working at the gym. He looked at me as if he didn't know me, but he knew exactly who I was. He said hello to me, as he did to everybody else, but he didn't make any reference at all to our fight. Tony is the kind of guy I find hard to fathom. He has a very quiet manner and it's difficult to know what he is thinking most of the time. Perhaps he is just shy. Or maybe the beating I handed him was a bit too painful for him to look back on.

Chapter 10

Alan

If I was to live my life again I would still want Alan to be my brother. By the same token, I would want my mum to be my mum. Not once, in all the times Alan had to go into hospital during his illness, did she miss a night at his bedside. She was always there to make sure that he was looked after properly, to comfort him and to hold his hand. I saw plenty of other kids who were suffering from the same disease in the hospital, but Alan was the only one who never had to endure those frightening nighttime hours alone. My mum was his angel, right until the very end.

The death of a child is the most traumatic event any us will ever be confronted with. Alan left us a few weeks after the Tony Tucker fight and, although we had known that he was nearing the end of his short life, it was still a huge shock for all of us when he passed away. It's hard to describe the feeling of utter devastation and loss we felt at that time. Heaven knows what we would have done without the help and support of those around us. There were so many, such as Paul and Sue, our friends from Lingwood, who were the first people to arrive at my mum's house, picking us up and taking us to the hospital, and Sue's mum, whom we affectionately knew as Supergran, who would drive over to visit Alan in his final weeks.

I was 15 when Alan came into the world. All I had ever wanted was a brother, and now I had one. It made me so proud. I was at boarding school and all I could talk about to the other boys was my little brother. From the moment he was born I was in awe of him and he felt the same way about me. To him I was a hero. Whatever anybody else had to say about me, I could do no wrong in his eyes. My old trainer, Jimmy McDonnell, once told me that, while he had seen brothers who were close, he had never seen brothers who were as close as Alan and I were.

Alan had been looking forward to watching me fight for the title and, thankfully, I was able to fulfil my promise of bringing the heavyweight title belt home to him. At first I hadn't wanted him to attend the Tucker fight because the cancer was at such an advanced stage by then and he was on medication just to control the pain. I was worried that the excitement might have been too much for him. In my mind, Tony was unlikely to give me a beating, but anything can happen in heavyweight boxing and, if I did walk onto a punch, I didn't want Alan to have to see it.

Of course, Alan didn't look at it that way. The possibility that I could lose this fight had never even entered his mind. We had a chat about it beforehand, and I explained to him that this was a serious fight for me,

When Bennt and I finally met in the ring there could be only one winner. I took his
BO heavyweight title in the seventh round.

Inset: I defended my WBO title against Riddick Bowe in Las Vegas. He stopped me in the sixth round.

After the Bowe fight I took some time out to build my dream house at Bawburgh a few miles outside Norwich.

Opposite: Time out from working on the Bawburgh house.

Above: My knockout of Tony Tucker in Norwich in 1997 was my best ever performance in the boxing ring. I knocked him out in the second round.

Below: Leaving the ring after the Tucker fight.

bove: Alan was with me every step of the way. Here we are at the post fight press onference with Frank Warren. A few weeks later his death left us devastated.

elow: I turned over a table at the press conference to announce my fight with italy Klitschko after Danny Williams, my sparring partner, claimed to have knocked e out in training. It was a long time before we were on speaking terms again.

The Hide clan: Henry is our eldest…

.Haley is the middle child...

...and here all the Hide kids – Henry, Haley and Hannah.

Alan

but it was no use. This was Alan's fight too, and he was determined to be there to cheer me on.

The only thing that kept me going during those weeks of training was the thought that I had to do this for Alan. He was deteriorating rapidly and this was my last chance to do something to make him happy. The preparation for the fight was awful. As I have already mentioned, there were a few lighter moments in the camp, but on the whole it was a particularly taxing time for me. Constantly trying to call my mother, for example, and not being able to get her because she was at the hospital with Alan was typical of the things that were going on in the background, taking their toll on me.

It wasn't only the fact that he was dying, but also the knowledge that Alan was suffering so terribly that was so upsetting for all of us. He was 11 years old and no child of that age should be burdened with that kind of pain. He had never done anything to hurt anybody and yet here was this illness that was taking over his young body.

Looking back at that time, I believe that I was in total denial of the situation. The doctors had made it clear that Alan was living on borrowed time but I stubbornly refused to accept that we would lose him. It just didn't seem real to me. Even now I have dreams that he is still alive, my little brother within touching distance.

There were so many emotions that I experienced during Alan's illness: despair, frustration and confusion. One of the most intense was the feeling of anger. This came to the fore after my accountant, the late Salman Suri, suggested that we take Alan to see a top specialist he knew in London. That specialist told us that, in his opinion, the treatment Alan had received in Norwich had been too aggressive for his leukaemia. I will always wonder whether Alan could have beaten the disease if he had been treated differently.

I remember discussing Alan's condition with the consultant in Norwich while Alan waited in the corridor outside. My mother and I felt that it would be wrong to tell Alan that he was going to die. He was so young and we didn't want to burden him with the terrible truth at that tender age. Besides, to look at him, you'd think there was nothing wrong, and we wanted him to enjoy the weeks and months he had left. The consultant felt differently.

'Are you out of your mind?' I asked him. 'If you dare to tell him, you will be dying with him.'

The consultant turned bright red. I had never felt this angry before in my whole life and I meant what I had said. If he had dared to go against our wishes, I would have been serving a life sentence for his murder now.

We believed that Alan could still be saved and we enlisted the services of a spiritual healer to help Alan. The healer was an Indian gentleman called Rishi, who had been recommended to us by Salman. He gave us something to hold onto when hope was all we had left. Rishi felt that he could cure Alan. He was convinced that, through the power of prayer, Alan would be able to cling to life and get better. By this stage Alan was confined to the hospital, rendered unconscious from the medication he was receiving, and we had no option but to believe what Rishi was telling us.

Rishi helped us greatly by brightening up our final days with Alan and giving us renewed hope but, in the end, his powers were not strong enough to save my little brother.

Alan

Perhaps he was just too ill and Rishi's efforts, while very much appreciated, were too little, too late.

Alan's good friend Robin was a huge source of support. I still talk to Robin all these years later and, in some ways, I think of him as another little brother. The two of them were so close and I had the feeling that Alan could share his darkest fears with Robin. One day I was at my mum's house while they were both playing. Alan had recently lost his hair as a result of the chemotherapy and, although it hadn't really occurred to me yet, he was very sensitive about it. In front of Robin this didn't seem to bother him, but Robin knew how embarrassed Alan felt about it. A group of boys arrived at the house to call on them. These were all friends of Alan's but he still wasn't comfortable letting them see his bare scalp. Robin saw them first and whispered to him that they had arrived. Alan was up like a shot, grabbing his hat and quickly pulling it on. Children of that age can be unkind and Alan clearly didn't want to be an object of ridicule. With Robin that was never the case. He was the only person outside of the immediate family whom Alan could really trust. Alan's death hit Robin very hard. He's a young adult now, part of our family. My kids never knew Alan, but in Robin they have a wonderful uncle.

Another great comfort for Alan came from a most unlikely source. I had hated the very sight of Michael Bentt in the weeks leading up to our fight but later I came to appreciate what a compassionate man he was. He and Alan struck up a beautiful friendship over the three years since Michael almost lost his life against me. They exchanged letters and phone calls from time to time and, when Alan turned ten, Michael sent him a dream catcher.

Nothing But Trouble

This is Native American creation, something that's hung over the bed to catch dreams and ward off anxiety. In Alan's case it seemed perfectly appropriate.

Michael was deeply touched by Alan's death and sent us a bouquet of flowers. Alan had a certain charisma about him and I think that's what Michael really came to appreciate. There was a kind of innocent charm to him and, although sometimes he would come across a bit cheeky, it was always in such an endearing way. He would speak his mind and was never afraid of anybody.

When we went to see my friend Francis Ampofo challenge Baby Jake Matlala for the WBO flyweight title at the Old York Hall in 1994, Alan would have been eight years old and I was still the undefeated WBO heavyweight champion. Lennox Lewis was enjoying his first stint as the WBC champion, so our names were sometimes linked in the media. His brother Dennis and manager Frank Maloney were also at the fight and they came over to say hello to us.

'Alan,' I said, 'this is Lennox Lewis's manager.'

Alan looked at them both and then answered, 'Lennox Lewis? He's crap.'

If *I* had said that, they might have found it quite offensive but, coming from Alan's young lips, it had us all laughing.

'Herbie, you're teaching that boy very well,' Frank told me.

Somebody else who had been impressed by Alan was Prince Naseem Hamed. While I had been training at the Wincobank Gym, Naz had admired my Mercedes S Series and came out with me for a spin. Alan called me on the car phone while we were driving and I passed him over.

Alan

Naz tried to talk to him in his gangster style and Alan had a good laugh with him. After hanging up, Naz enquired how old Alan was. When I told him, he couldn't believe it. He thought that Alan sounded so mature and sensible, well beyond his years. Naz was another one, like Michael Bentt and so many others, who sent us flowers.

Alan always knew that, if he wanted anything, he could come to me. The deal was, if he needed pocket money, he would give me that number of kisses. I was always good for a tenner if he would show me some affection. One time he came to me and said, 'I need some money.'

'How much?' I asked him.

'Fifty pounds.' He was going into town with Robin and he wanted to make a good impression.

'Fifty quid? Well, you know what you have to do.'

He kissed me about five times and then disappeared with the money. I could hear Robin in the background saying, 'Easy money.'

That happy-go-lucky aura had deserted him by the time of the Tucker fight. I had hoped that he would enjoy it but, later when I watched the bout again on television, I realised that he had been incredibly nervous about the outcome. Because he was so young, I had assumed that he wouldn't really understand how important the fight was, how much was riding on it for me – emotionally as well as professionally. He understood though; he understood completely.

When he joined me at the press conference afterwards, it was the final time I saw Alan as I knew him. That was when I gave him the belt. He left with Helen. She told me afterwards that they had been to see her parents first and that he had been enjoying himself there, trying the belt on Chico, the German Shepherd that Helen and I had given her mum and dad as a present.

Later that evening I went back to my mum's house and Alan was also home, lying on the floor of his bedroom watching the fight again on video. I sat down beside him and he didn't look at me. In fact, he never looked at me again after that.

Although we hadn't spoken to him about it, Alan knew that he was dying. Once I had beaten Tucker it seemed as though there was nothing left for him to hang on to. His condition deteriorated quickly until, six weeks later, he left us. I buried him with the belt.

My mum and I were inconsolable. I am sure that my dad must have felt the same but, on the outside at least, he seemed to cope with the loss better.

Death comes to all of us sooner or later, and Alan's time had arrived. His life was short and beautiful, and his passing is something I will never come to terms with, although it does get easier with the passage of time. Alan was so perfect in every way and, while I have three beautiful children of my own now who mean the world to me, I don't think I will ever share the kind of relationship with them that I had with my brother. Alan was more than my best friend: he was, and still is, my soulmate.

Chapter 11

Picking up the Pieces

Even though I am not a football fan, I knew about the Fashanu brothers, Justin and John, from my earliest days in Norwich and, while I didn't have any direct contact with either of them, Gordon Holmes, a local boxing manager who looked after the likes of Marty Duke, Richard Bustin, Danny Porter and Dave Lawrence in the early 1990s, knew them quite well. There were several similarities: they were sporting Nigerians who had been adopted and both had connections with Norwich. That was why I looked up to them as a youngster.

It was years later, once I had won the title against Tony Tucker, when John approached me about becoming my manager. We met in the Hilton Hotel in Abuja to talk about it and, although I made it clear that I didn't really need a manager as such, I was quite happy to work with him if he was able to secure me more endorsements.

John has a certain way about him. He looks very smart

and he articulates himself very well. These were qualities that I thought might be able to help me. John was still trying to put his career back together after being tried for, and acquitted of, fixing football matches in 1997.

He met with Frank Warren, and Warren was happy enough to have him on board if he could deliver what he promised. The deal was that John would get 10 per cent of any income he could generate through endorsements, although I suspect that Warren also saw John as a means of breaking into the football world. There was talk of a deal with Nigerian television, in which they would pay to show my fights, but it came to nothing. After that, John and I drifted apart.

I was still cordial with Frank Warren although, for me, it was purely a business relationship. Sometimes we would share a joke, like the time I told him that my accountant, Salman Suri, had been murdered in a hotel in Bulgaria and he said, 'You're kidding. I gave him £25,000 for you last week.' That was as far is it went between us though and we never came close to approaching the same sort of relationship which Barry and I shared. Everything I did while we were working together had a financial reason behind it. We had one or two disagreements on the monetary side of things and, as is often the case where cash is involved, our relationship went downhill from there.

Some would say that letting me fight for the title in my home city, giving me the platform to provide Alan with that last precious experience, was the greatest favour that Warren could have done for me. I would agree: being able to win the title like that meant the world to me and I was grateful for the opportunity. At the same time,

Picking up the Pieces

Warren wasn't doing it for free, and nor was I. As the promoter, he stood to make a profit from staging the event. For me, as a prize fighter, I was to be paid accordingly for headlining the show.

With Barry, a young fighter knows that he is going to be paid, provided Barry thinks that the boxer is worth the investment in the long term. That's not to say that a prospect will be set up for life but, as long as the money he receives is enough to get by on, he can concentrate on what is important – training. That's how it was for me when I first joined the professional ranks. Money was sometimes tight but I was a full-time fighter with no other distractions, and that was what enabled me to improve and develop. A young guy needs to be paid every week in order to continue as a full-time professional. As long as you have a regular income, you are OK but, if you find yourself waiting for your wages and the bills still need to be paid, you get frustrated. Once you decide to get a job, even if it's only part time, then you are unable to concentrate on your boxing in the way you would have done before.

Warren has brought some classy guys through from the start of their professional careers. People like Ricky Hatton and Amir Khan had always been with Warren, but in both cases they were outstanding amateurs who already had a lot of support. For those guys the ticket sales were guaranteed so it wasn't such a risk backing them. When I turned professional I had only a very brief amateur career behind me, and I didn't have anything like the contacts or the backing that Hatton and Khan enjoyed. There was no guarantee for Barry that I would become successful so it was a risk for him to back me the

139

way he did. I am incredibly thankful to Barry for that because it was his belief in me that enabled me to achieve what I have. I don't think Warren would have had as much faith in me.

There was one occasion when I needed about £80,000 from him so that I could buy a new Porsche. This was money I had already earned and I was just waiting for him to make good on the payment. He arranged for me to meet him in a hotel so that I could collect the money from him there. I went along with a friend because I wanted to pick up the Porsche as soon as I had collected the cash, and somebody needed to drive the Range Rover back for me. My friend was asked to wait outside while I went in to collect the money. When you see that amount of cash all in one place it looks like a fortune. Before he handed over the money, Warren had said that he knew the car dealer and that I could get him to send the bill and he would pay it. I knew the dealer too, and he said no. He was adamant that he wanted payment before he released the car to me.

It has been said that my first defence of the title, a first-round stoppage of Damon Reed in April 1998, was a complete waste of time. Well, I stopped in him 52 seconds, so it was easy for journalists to jump on the bandwagon and write that he was never any good in the first place.

Those same journalists claimed that I wasn't ready for a decent challenge. They said that it was too soon after Alan's death and that my state of mind was too fragile. In hindsight, that's a lot of rubbish. I'm a fighter and it's my job to fight whoever is put in front of me, win or lose.

Picking up the Pieces

Alan's death still hurts now, more than a decade later, so if you follow that line of thinking I would *never* be ready to return to the ring. Several months had gone by and I was ready to fight again.

Reed, who came from Kansas in the USA, looked like a cruiserweight. He was 6ft (1.8m) tall, which is very small for a fighter in the heavyweight division and, at 14st 10lb (93kg), he weighed almost a stone (6.3kg) less than I did. The truth is, though, he was a good fighter. Maybe he was not world class, but as a cruiserweight he could have achieved a lot more than he did at heavyweight. That said, he had lost only once, against 22 wins, before we met. That was by decision over eight rounds against Brian Nielsen in Denmark. Whatever people wanted to say about him, he wasn't a bum.

This was my last fight with Jimmy and, as was always the case when Jimmy had been training me, I was in fantastic shape. I was ready to fight 50 rounds with him if necessary, but got the job done in a little more than 50 seconds. I went straight after him and staggered him with a right hook after about 15 seconds. I followed up with another right and then put him down with my left hand. The referee let him continue but, as soon as I attacked him with a hard right cross, he held on for dear life and the referee had to stop the fight. That was the fastest heavyweight title fight ever. It's a record I still hold and one I'm very proud of.

Reed has lost a few more fights since then, but he has faced one or two decent heavyweights, guys such as Kali Meehan and Monte Barrett, who have both fought for versions of the title themselves, and nobody has stopped him in the first round. Perhaps the people who wrote those things then should now give me a bit of credit.

The following month I attended a boxing show at the Prince Regent Hotel in Chigwell. As well as the boxing, an auction had been organised for Francis Ampofo, who needed to raise money for his son, Samson. Samson is wonderful, happy boy. He is also autistic and he needed to go on a course, where he would benefit from the Lovaas method of therapy for afflicted children, whereby they undergo one-on-one teaching, the cost of which was £20,000 a year (it's named after the clinical psychologist Ole Ivar Lovaas). People wanted to help Samson and I agreed to put my first WBO belt up for sale. It was a very tough decision, but one that I think was worth making, as the belt sold for £7,000 to John 'Goldfinger' Palmer, the Tenerife timeshare magnate who was jailed for fraud in 2001. Francis was delighted.

It had been clear to me for a while that my professional relationship with Jimmy had run its course and, after the Reed fight, it was time for us to go our separate ways. Let's return to the Bowe fight for a moment. Jimmy turned down an offer of £50,000 to act as my conditioner. That was as much as he earned for the Azumah Nelson fight, and all he had to do was look after my fitness, but it wasn't enough.

Of course, Freddie stood to earn a good bit more from the fight but that was only fair: he had taught me everything I knew in the professional game and there was no reason to demote him for the biggest fight of my career.

There was a guy who helped out in the gym called Patsy. He would look after these little tasks that the trainer would normally undertake. While we were preparing for the Tucker fight Patsy did so much to assist Jimmy and to make me feel at ease. He's one of those unsung heroes of the sport, those who will never have their names up in lights but are greatly appreciated by those who do. Jimmy earned £19,000 as my trainer for that fight after collecting 10 per cent of my purse. Added to that was his cut for training Scott Welsh and Joe Bugner Jr on the same show. All in all, it was a very lucrative evening for him. I was disgusted when I heard that Patsy hadn't received any financial recognition for the part he played.

Jimmy can say he masterminded Danny Williams' victory over Mike Tyson in 2004, but he should look at why Danny would want to train with him in the first place. Danny worked as my sparring partner when I was training with Jimmy, and I would knock him all over the place. As a trainer, the best way to impress a promising boxer is to let your boy beat him up. That's what attracted him to Jimmy – he thought Jimmy must have been doing something right with me.

But Jimmy has a lot of good points too. His humour is infectious and he used to have me in stitches when he spoke. When we were training I really enjoyed being around him. He was also an incredible motivator. It was impossible not to feel positive about what you were doing when Jimmy was training you. If Jimmy was to turn up on my doorstep I would welcome him in with open arms. It's just that, as a championship-level fighter, I felt it was time to move on.

Once the Reed fight was out of the way, I was due to face my first mandatory contender. The WBO informed me that this would be Willi Fischer from Germany. However, before that could go ahead there was a little bit of legal trouble that needed to be cleared up. I was due at Norwich Crown Court to answer two charges of assault, which had allegedly taken place a year and a half previously, when I was in the early stages of my preparation for the Tucker fight.

Like many of my little problems with the Norwich police, I believed that this was a storm in a teacup and should never have resulted in a court appearance. But the police didn't want to see it that way, and nor did my accuser.

The Norwich Lads' Club had moved to the Kickstop gym on Whiffler Road. They celebrated their new opening in March 1997 and on the first day I had been training there with Graham Everett. The deal was that the professionals would train during the day and then, in the evening, the amateur boxers would have their turn.

Some of the amateur trainers felt uncomfortable when I was around. Without blowing my own trumpet, I was a world-class heavyweight and a former world champion while many of these guys, although very committed, were nothing more than well-meaning volunteers. They came to the gym because they loved the sport and because they wanted to help the kids, but when those kids saw me training they would watch what I was doing, how I was training, and this would undermine the guys who gave up their time to coach them. It wasn't as if I wanted to irritate the coaches like this – I always minded my own business when I was in the gym – but it just had this effect.

Training has a lot to do with ego. People wanted to

believe that they created me, the same as they wanted to believe that they were moulding the current crop of youngsters. It wasn't really like that though. You cannot build a heavyweight champion from scratch. I was already very athletic when I first came to the club, and fighting was instinctive for me. There were people there who helped me reach a decent standard but it was later, under Freddie King at Matchroom, that I started to learn about combinations and things like that.

When I was young I was very shy, I stuttered whenever I spoke and I didn't socialise very well. People felt sorry for me but they knew that I could fight and they were happy to have me around. When people take pity on you they are also looking down on you and this gives them a feeling of safety, that they are in a position where they can afford to help you because they are better off. That fact is I outgrew the Lads' Club. I liked being around the place and I still have a lot of friends there, but I was the boy who made it to the top level.

Once I turned professional and started winning things I was suddenly more important than the people who had been able to pat me on the head and say, 'Well done, Herbie!' Nobody could feel sorry for me after that, and various members of the club didn't like it.

On this day I had arrived late at the gym, meaning that my training session overran. I was still working away when a guy I knew, Ali Drummond, and a guy I didn't, Chris Johnson, came into the gym. I hadn't really noticed them because I had been so wrapped up in my own programme, but they were there to train the youngsters. My ghetto blaster was also turned up loud so that I could listen to Michael Jackson while I was working out, so I wouldn't necessarily have heard them come in.

Ali came over and turned off my music. It wasn't a big deal because I knew he wasn't taking a liberty. Ali and I had known each other for years and we would always mess about when we were in the gym together. I went over to him and tripped him up. Ali knew that I was only playing, and that I didn't mean any harm, but another guy there got the wrong end of the stick. The cheeky sod came over to me and smacked me. What was I supposed to do? I didn't even know this guy and he had just attacked me in front of everybody in the gym. I hit him back, but it was only self-defence.

Les King was also there that evening and he saw what happened. As it escalated he asked me to leave, which was correct because I was really annoyed by now and the last thing the club needed was a fight in front of the kids. The police were brought in and people made statements, but Les, out of loyalty to me, refused to follow suit.

The guy I fought with knew that I was well known, and he also knew that I had a few quid in the bank, so when he called me a few days later to say that he would retract all of his allegations if I was to give him a £30,000 out-of-court settlement I knew that I was being set up.

There were a couple of reasons why I never gave him the money. The first was that I was innocent. He had started the trouble, so I saw no reason why I should be paying him compensation. The second was that Ronnie Brookes, who also worked as a magistrate, had advised me to record my calls. I did this, meaning that I had proof that he was trying to get money. The charges of assault occasioning actual bodily harm were dropped when the other guy failed to show up at the court. It wasn't the first time that someone had tried to get cash out of me.

I had been seeing a girl years before. When I say seeing, I mean we got together once or twice. We were never serious about each other but we remained on friendly terms and would meet up from time to time over the next couple of years. Then she started going out with a nasty piece of work who would beat her up, but whom she still carried on seeing anyway. While she was with him she carried on visiting me at my home to chat. He was a very jealous sort and wasn't at all happy about her seeing me.

One evening when I was out in Norwich I saw her in a nightclub and went over to say hello. I didn't even know who the man with her was at this point, never mind that he was a boyfriend, so I was quite surprised when he came up to me punched me in the head. Of course, I hit him back and we finished up brawling with each other. The police charged me with assault after he called them. He wanted her to testify against me, to say that I had started the fight, but she refused. She turned up at my house to tell me, black and blue from the hiding he had given her.

Then he called me, claiming that I should give him £5,000 to drop the charges. This is when I called Ronnie. I had never had anybody demanding money from me before and it made me very uneasy. His answer was simple: 'Tape the next call!' Sure enough, he called back. Again he told me that he wanted the £5,000, adding that the Norwich police were in on this and that they were going to take a portion of that money for themselves. I recorded all of this.

There was no truth in that last statement whatsoever.

Still, the case was taken out of the Norfolk Constabulary's hands and referred to the police force in London. Once they had the tapes they were able to see through his plan immediately. My name was cleared and he finished up serving six months for blackmail. It just goes to show, there are people out there who are willing to stoop to any level to get their hands on other people's money. It's strange but after he came out of prison I started to get on reasonably well with him. I certainly wouldn't class him as a friend, but if I saw him in town I would stop to have a chat with him.

Perhaps blackmail is an occupational hazard. I don't know. What I do know is that the business taught me a valuable lesson. Even though I felt sure that there was really no case to answer, I was glad to be able to put the matter behind me and concentrate on Willi Fischer. He had been a decent amateur who represented Germany in the Barcelona Olympics. As a professional he had knocked out most of his opponents, losing only once, although virtually all his fights had taken place in Germany. There weren't really any top-drawer fighters on his record but the WBO still wanted to give him a chance, so he came over to Norwich to fight me.

He wasn't any trouble. As I would have expected against a fighter of his calibre, I walked through him with relative ease. The most difficult thing, probably for both of us, was the leaking roof above our heads, which was causing water to fall onto the canvas. Willi was able to cope with some of my heavy shots in the first round and the crowd probably thought it would turn into a long fight, but that changed in the second when I floored him with a combination of two jabs, a right and a left hook. It was so fast that he had no answer for it.

I floored him a second time with a beautifully timed left hook but somehow he managed to get up again. After the third knockdown, which followed another four-punch combination, the referee, Joe Cortez, waved it off.

A boxer can fight only the man standing in front of him and, in all honesty, Willi Fischer was not the kind of quality opponent for whom a champion will be remembered. I did a job on him, and I think I put on an impressive show, but my career now desperately needed to be ratcheted up a notch or two with a fight against a top-level challenger.

Chapter 12

Money to Burn

There is no way that Danny Williams would ever beat me if we were to meet in the ring. He's a talented enough fighter, judged on his own merits, but he doesn't share my abilities. He had his moment of glory in 2004, when he stopped Mike Tyson in four rounds in Louisville but, by this time, Iron Mike was a long way past his sell-by date and was fighting for the money. Danny had already lost fights against ordinary heavyweights, such as Britain's Julius Francis and Sinan Samil Sam from Turkey, so Tyson must have mistakenly believed that, even with his own diminished skills, Danny would be easy prey. This victory was the highlight of Danny's career. Tyson is a nice name to have on your ring record, but Danny has never really fulfilled his early potential and he certainly hasn't succeeded at world level.

He was taking a huge liberty when he claimed, at the press conference to promote my match with the Ukrainian giant Vitali Klitschko in June 1999, that he could beat me. What's more, he told the assembled journalists that he had knocked me out in training while we were sparring together. He was employed as my sparring partner and he should have shown more respect than to undermine me in public like that. The upshot was that I lost my temper, turned over a table and told Danny exactly what I thought of him. It used to make my blood boil when I thought about it.

It's a shame, because Danny was a nice guy and somebody I was happy to work with, but he overstepped the mark at that press conference. Perhaps he believed that one day he would be the world champion himself, but that was never very likely. After this episode Danny wasn't safe anywhere near me. If I had been left alone in a room with him I think I would have ripped him limb from limb.

So what exactly happened that day against Danny Williams in sparring? The answer is that Danny got lucky. He knows, and I know, that when we were sparring together I would beat him up every day and twice on Sunday. It was as if he was coming to my church and I was giving him the sermon. Then one day he caught me with a good punch and I went down. These things can happen in boxing if you don't concentrate, and Danny managed to hit me with a decent shot. I was so angry that I got up and gave him a beating as never before, as if he had taken something from me that didn't belong to him. If you had seen us in the ring at that point you would have thought that he had stolen my bike.

When he claimed to have knocked me out, in front of all those journalists at the press conference, I challenged him, saying, 'Look me in the eye and tell me that you knocked me out,' I told him.

He didn't move. He knew at that moment that he was in trouble.

'Danny,' I repeated, 'look me in the eye and tell me that you knocked me out.'

Jimmy McDonnell, who was now Danny's trainer, told him to look at me. People were laughing by this stage. Danny turned to me and looked at me briefly. That's when I flipped the table over. As far as I was concerned, by making eye contact he was demonstrating a complete and utter lack of respect. I went looking for him but by the time I got outside the room he was nowhere to be found. It says something about the difference between us though. Danny is just a big guy who boxes, while I am a born fighter.

After that press conference Warren wanted me to take part in a public sparring session. I told him that it would be no problem, provided he got Danny as the sparring partner so I could show the world that he had absolutely nothing on me. Obviously, Danny didn't want to know. Heaven only knows what Vitali thought. He was the mandatory challenger for the title but all anybody could talk about in the lead-up to the fight was the altercation between Danny and me.

There were four of us – Nigel Brightwell, Graham Everett, Neil Featherby and I – who travelled back to Norwich that evening. We were in my Bentley, travelling along the A11 listening to Kenny Rogers singing 'Ruby, Don't Take Your Love to Town', which I liked even if the others didn't. Graham was at the wheel and I was sitting beside him, which made what happened next all the more frightening. We were driving along in single file when Graham decided to overtake a lorry in front of us. He must have forgotten that the Bentley is like a tank and takes ages to pick up speed, and before we knew it there was another lorry bearing down on us from the opposite direction. We all sat there looking at this huge machine heading directly at us, praying that the Bentley was going to accelerate enough to get past this lorry, which had been slower than we were going when we were behind it, but which now seemed to be moving at exactly the same speed.

Somehow Graham managed to get up enough power to move past it and back into our lane. We missed the oncoming lorry with only inches to spare. All four of us had thought we were going to die, there and then. I was gripping the sides of my seat so hard that my knuckles had turned white.

We sat silently for about half a minute, wondering how in the world we had avoided that truck. Then I said, 'I don't mind telling you, I shit myself.'

The others just burst out laughing.

'Cor, boy,' Nigel said in his best Norfolk accent, 'I thought we were all brown bread.'

That wasn't the only time we nearly lost our lives on that stretch of road during those six weeks of preparation. Throughout the week we based ourselves in Hendon and returned to Norwich at the weekends. Every Sunday night we would meet up and drive back together so that we could start training again on the Monday morning.

One Sunday evening Neil and Graham arrived at my house with another sparring partner, Nate Tubbs, at 7pm. It took me a bit longer to get myself sorted out, but by 1.30am we were ready to leave. I sat in the front passenger seat beside Neil, who was driving, with Graham and Nate sitting in the back. All of a sudden, as we were passing Thetford, we felt the car veering to the right, into the path of an oncoming car. Neil had fallen asleep at the wheel. We were yelling and shouting at him to wake up before he got us all killed. It was another close call and we had to stop at a petrol station so that he could get a couple of pints of black coffee down his neck. He spent the rest of that trip laughing to himself about nearly crashing the car.

Vitali is probably more famous for a fight he lost than any of those he actually won. In 2003 he suffered terrible cuts in a challenge to Lennox Lewis for the WBC title after stepping in as a late substitute for the injured Kirk Johnson. He posed Lennox a few problems in the early rounds, but by the middle of the fight Lennox was starting to find his range and almost destroyed Vitali with a monstrous uppercut. Vitali had been leading on the scorecards but I think Lennox would have stopped him sooner rather than later if the cuts had not made it impossible for Vitali to continue. The Americans loved him for his bravery, just as they had loved me for my performance against Riddick Bowe, and before long he was rewarded with another shot at the title. Lennox decided to retire after that fight so Vitali squared off against the South African Corrie Sanders for the vacant title. Sanders had flattened Vitali's younger brother, Wladimir, in his previous fight and looked like doing the same to Vitali, staggering him early on before Vitali took control to win the title in the eighth round. Some felt that

Vitali would go on to be a great champion, but he managed only one defence of the belt, when he stopped Danny Williams in 2004.

But that was still in the future when we met in London in June 1999. After two voluntary defences I was due a mandatory challenger, and the WBO had chosen the still unbeaten Vitali for me. He was big at 6ft 6in, and powerful, having won all 27 of his fights inside the distance, but he hadn't fought anybody above trial-horse level. Basically, he was still untested.

I went in with Klitschko having not fought since beating Willi Fischer the previous September. A fight that had been organised against Orlin Norris, the former WBA cruiserweight champion – who was now campaigning as a heavyweight – which should actually have taken place the previous year but then fell through when Orlin injured his knee, was rearranged for February 1999 in Newcastle. It would have been my next fight after Fischer but I was forced to withdraw because I had developed a horrible rash. My skin was itching terribly and had developed a bumpy texture. I was scratching at it frantically, so much so that I was making myself bleed. There was no real reason for it, other than stress. I was still coming to terms with losing Alan and I believe that this was probably the root of it. Eventually, it went away of its own accord, but it was enough to make me call off the fight.

The match against Orlin was doomed. We thought it was finally going to take place in April on a bill in London but then I injured my Achilles tendon and was forced to pull out again. By this time the WBO were getting a bit tetchy and told me that it was time to face a mandatory contender, otherwise they would strip me of the belt. For Orlin it was very bad luck. He never did get the chance to fight for the heavyweight title but at least he was able to appear on the bill in London, where he stopped Pele Reid in the first round.

That Achilles injury was still troubling me when I attended the press conference to announce the fight with Klitschko. I think I aggravated it while I had been doing fitness training with Neil Featherby. We had been running on roads and that kind of injury is just an unfortunate thing that can happen on hard surfaces.

To be honest, it was probably possible to organise other fights for me before I faced Klitschko but that wasn't my only problem – money was a bit of an issue in my life too, after I was made bankrupt. When I was in my mid-20s, with a big house, several cars and more dosh than I could possibly spend, I didn't know the first thing about bankruptcy. Like most people who have never experienced it, I thought that bankruptcy was a means to an end for those who have lost control of their finances. For me there were no spiralling debts, no creditors looking for payments I couldn't make, and no bank manager who had lost patience with my inability to keep my head above water. I had nothing to worry about, or so I thought.

The courts declared me bankrupt because I refused to pay a bill. This was after I sent my Mercedes in to be repaired after it developed a problem with the air conditioning. I thought it would have been a simple procedure to put it right but when the car came back I was still not happy with it. They still wanted about

Nothing But Trouble

£1,200 from me and I wasn't willing to pay. It's amazing that something like that can happen.

While I was training for Klitschko, I was staying at my flat in Hendon with Graham and Neil. We wanted to be near London and the flat was in a handy location. I have known Neil for several years and I consider him to be a very good friend of mine. He already knew Graham well from the sports scene in Norwich, but I was the one who first approached him when I suggested that we could work together. I had seen the way he trained Jon Thaxton and the kickboxer Gary Briggs, getting them in superb condition, and I hoped he could do something similar for me. At first he declined. He felt that he had enough to do with Jon and Gary, and with his other business interests.

Neil has his fingers in several pies. He runs a successful sports shop on the Drayton Business Park, on the outskirts of Norwich. As well as this, he is involved in the management of several athletes, including me, Jon Thaxton and various footballers. However, it is for his running abilities that he first became well known. In the 1990s he represented Great Britain and England at the World Athletics Cup and the European Cup as a long-distance runner. His personal best for the marathon is 2 hours, 17 minutes, so he certainly knows a thing or two about fitness and conditioning. He also has a wicked sense of humour and can wind me up mercilessly.

It was thanks to Neil that I didn't lose a considerable amount of money through my own carelessness. Having been declared bankrupt I wasn't able to use my bank accounts the way I normally would. For this reason I had a certain amount of cash with me to keep me going while I was training. The money was wrapped up in one of those cloth bags from the bank and one evening when I went out I left it hidden inside the lightshade in my bedroom. It was one of those upturned metal shades that hang from the ceiling, so nobody would have been able to see it there. I thought it would be a safe place, and it probably would have been if the light hadn't been switched on. Actually, I could smell something burning before I left the house but I just assumed that it was a barbecue from a nearby garden.

Neil and Graham, who had been out having something to eat when I left the flat, arrived back before I did and sat down in the living room, where they watched television and made some calls. As they were about to go to bed Neil said he could smell something burning. It's a good thing he noticed it because otherwise the whole flat might have gone up in flames. They opened the door to my room and almost choked as the thick smoke billowed out. Neil said to Graham, 'Check the plugs!' and off Graham went to have a look in the bath and the sink. It sounds like a daft thing to do, but then he was probably completely shocked by the situation and not thinking straight.

'What are you doing?' Neil said. 'I meant the plugs on the walls.' It didn't matter because he had found the source of the smoke by then. The lightshade was so hot that it was turning red while the bag was smouldering away to virtually nothing. The £8,000 worth of £20 notes it had been holding looked to be useless.

When I arrived back I could immediately see what had happened. I sat down in all the ash on my bedroom floor and tried to take it in. 'Well,' I said to them, 'worse things have happened to me before.'

Nothing But Trouble

Neil took those charred notes to the bank for me and, fortunately, he was able to get most of them replaced. What we thought was going to be a write-off of £8,000 turned into a loss of just £80. Those last four charred £20 notes are pasted to the ceiling of SportLink, his sports shop in Drayton.

That wasn't the only time Neil helped me out of a sticky situation during that training camp. There was one occasion when his quick thinking saved us a great deal of embarrassment and several difficult questions. We had been to the African restaurant and were strolling back to the flat at about 11 o'clock when we heard a woman groaning. Where we were walking there was a huge hedge separating the pavement from an adjoining park and the noises we could hear were coming from the other side. We both rushed to the nearest entrance to the park and quickly found where the woman was lying. The lady, who had clearly been smacked about before we found her, was lying on a bowling green, out of her face. She kept begging us to help her, so we picked her up and helped her out of the park and onto the street. Then, all of a sudden, she became very wary of Neil.

'Get off me!' she told him. 'You're a copper.'

'I'm not a copper. We're just trying to help you,' he told her.

While he was saying that she pulled away from him and, in her drunken state, she landed on her head. We picked her up again and she kept saying to me, 'You have to help me, but don't let the copper nick me.'

There were a couple of things she could have been nicked for, including being out of her head on alcohol and drugs, but what she was afraid of was being arrested for prostitution. It had already been a bad night for her, with one of her punters doing her over, and an evening in the cells wouldn't have made things any better.

Once we got her as far as Hendon High Street a police car drove past, taking a long, hard look at the three of us. If that had been in Norwich they would have pulled me in immediately but in Hendon the police never caused me any bother.

We were soon distracted from the police car by a bloke who walked towards us, also a bit the worse for wear, who noticed me.

'Are you Herbie Hide?'

'Yes, I am,' I said, standing there trying to prop up this paralytic hooker, as if it were the most normal thing in the world, and appear polite at the same time.

'I can't believe it. I've just met Herbie Hide. I'm a big fan of yours.'

While I was trying not to get dragged into a conversation with this well-meaning but poorly timed fan, Neil had his eye on what was happening further down the street. The police car had stopped a hundred yards further on and they were watching us quite intently.

'Listen, mate,' Neil said to our new friend. 'Would you like to do Herbie here a big favour?'

'Of course I would,' he said.

'OK then. You see this lady? She's in a bad way and could do with some medical help. There's a police car over there. Maybe you could help her over to them for us.'

With that they both staggered off in the direction of the police car. He was trying to make conversation with her while she was oblivious of everything he said. I have no idea what happened, although I suspect the young lady was taken into the station. It saved me a lot of trouble though because, if word of this had got out, I could have been back in the press, this time for allegedly beating up prostitutes. We were only trying to help somebody out, but if the story had reached the papers I am sure some people wouldn't have believed our side of events.

My first child, Henry, also came into the world while I was training for the Klitschko fight. We had a call one morning at 5.15 from Helen to say that he had been born and, later that evening, after we had been training at Hampstead Heath, the three of us drove over to Norwich. Neil was at the wheel when one of the tyres blew on the M11 and we had to pull over. Both Graham and I thought that it was a joke at first. I waited in the car with Graham while Neil ran off to find an SOS phone.

'What would you have done if you'd been on your own and the tyre had blown?' Neil asked me as we were waiting for the RAC to arrive.

'I wouldn't have stopped,' I told him. 'I would have carried on driving.'

'Why's that then?'

'Because we're in the middle of nowhere and it's dark. I'm not going out there with all those ghosts around.' That was it. Neil had discovered one of my major weaknesses and he started telling one ghost story after the other. I was screaming and Graham wasn't much better. At one point, through sheer terror, he jumped so high in the back seat that he smashed his head on the roof. Neil thought all of this was hilarious and since then he has often tried to frighten me. My problem is that I always listen to him when I should ignore him.

Money to Burn

Training for the Klitschko fight could have been much better. John Hornewer had asked me to prepare for the fight in America and, in hindsight, maybe it would have been a good idea. I would certainly have been sparring with some quality fighters – men such as Lance Whittaker, the huge heavyweight, who would have replicated Klitschko's size, and Ross Puritty, who had beaten Klitschko's younger brother, Wladimir.

Instead, I chose to stay in England. The quality of sparring I needed was very thin on the ground. I remember that I worked with Nate Tubbs and the late James Oyebola for a week or so. I was often glad to have anybody there at all who would spar with me, such as the time a really tall fella called Danny Watts came into the gym looking for some work. When he got into the ring with me I hit him with a left hook, which put his nose completely out of joint. I had never seen anything like it – I thought that his nose had come off. He needed an operation to put that right. It was probably the worst injury I have ever seen in a boxing gym.

When the sparring partners did come it was my responsibility to pay them. I had one guy, an American heavy called Lynwood Jones, who came back to the flat with us from the Lennox Lewis Academy one evening after I forgot to bring the cash to pay him. He didn't bother getting changed at all, he just had on what he had been wearing in the gym – shorts and boots – and crammed himself into the back seat of the car. Once we were back in Hendon I gave him his money and he was quite happy. Neil was the one who had to walk him to the train station so that he could catch the Tube back to London. It was rush hour on a Friday afternoon and

163

there were people everywhere on Hendon High Street, all of them looking at Neil with this half-naked American. Lyndon was big around the belly as well. Neil was just glad to see that back of him.

We also did some open sparring for the media at Canary Wharf where I knocked out Ray Austin. Warren was furious with me for that. As he saw it, I should have been using the sparring to practise my moves rather than beat people up. I thought that he should have kept his mouth shut. I should also point out that I love beating people up in sparring, just as I love hurting people in a proper boxing match. That is how I fight and Warren should have known it before he organised the session. As I see it, I stand to get hurt if I don't attack the other guy first.

Even though Klitschko beat me when we met in London, I didn't rate him as a fighter. I didn't think he was any good then, after he stopped me, and I still don't think he's anything special now. To me, he's just a big, strong guy. All he had over me was a big advantage in size. You have to remember that, for all the fights I fought at heavyweight, I was really just a blown-up cruiserweight. When a heavyweight like that hits me I will fall. Klitschko weighed in at 17st 8lb for that fight, while my weight was just 15st 11bs. That was an advantage of nearly two stone – a lot for a guy who can hit incredibly hard anyway.

Brendan Ingle was back in my corner on the evening of the fight. Warren never really liked having Graham training me and he thought it was a much safer bet for Brendan to take control during the fight. I think the world of Brendan. He is such an outstanding trainer and I was happy to have him there with me at the London

Arena. I have to say, though, that Brendan couldn't help me in the way I would have hoped in this fight. Being out of the ring for so long had certainly had an effect on me, and after the first round I felt flustered. Klitschko was difficult to hit and I started to feel uncomfortable. I think Brendan should have realised this and used his experience to calm me down, get me to stay out of Klitschko's way and let him do all the work until I had found my rhythm. Once I was settled I could have buckled down and completed the job correctly. Instead, he told me to go back out there, step to the side and crack Klitschko with my right hand. Out of respect for Brendan, I tried to do it, but I knew it wasn't going to work for me at this early stage of the fight.

In the second round Klitschko hit me in the eye and I had great difficulty even seeing what was standing in front of me, never mind fighting back. I wanted to fight the right kind of fight, but I couldn't, and then I got nailed with a left jab and a right hand from Klitschko. When the same thing happened again a minute or so later I was counted out.

It's annoying because this was a fighter I could have, and should have, beaten. Klitschko's boxing skills were very basic and, if I had managed to take the fight into the later rounds, I am sure that I would have won it. But these things don't always go your way, so you have to accept them and move on. The heavyweight division was looking wide open after Lennox Lewis and Evander Holyfield had managed only to draw their first fight, and there would have been so many opportunities open to me if I hadn't stumbled against Klitschko. A fight with Mike Tyson might even have been possible at last, but it wasn't to be.

Chapter 13

Trouble with the Law

Not all of the police in Norwich are bad. One or two of them are decent, respectable people. I realised this when I was arrested for allegedly raping somebody a few years ago. It was around the time that Mike Tyson came over to England in January 2000 for his fight against Julius Francis in Manchester.

This police officer had pulled me over a few weeks beforehand, demanding to see my documents. The police know that this gets on my nerves, but there is nothing I can do about it. They see my car and something sounds in their brain. Helen, who was with me in the car, was as fed up as I was about the whole situation. 'I'm sick and tired of this,' she told him. 'How are we supposed to drive anywhere? Every time you see a car with Herbie Hide inside it you pull us over.'

The policeman said nothing and I thought Helen was wasting her breath.

When the complaint was made the police brought me

to the station for questioning. I didn't know who the girl was, but when an allegation like this is made they have to act on it. They had me there for two and a half days, asking me questions and doing medical tests. I remember one of them referring to her as the 'victim'. 'Hold on a minute,' I said. 'Did you just call her the victim? The victim is sitting here in front of you. The victim has been here for days answering your questions about a rape that never even took place and about a woman he's never even met, let alone had sex with.'

You can imagine that I was in a pretty bad mood. When the police officer who had stopped me with Helen a few weeks previously came to me between questioning, I thought that things were just about to take a turn for the worse. 'I just want to wish you good luck with this case,' he said. He didn't need to say any more than that. I knew from that moment that he could see the allegations were ridiculous and suddenly I had a warm sensation in my chest. This guy was a human being.

Some of the older police officers were OK. They would have a joke with me when I came in, but most of the younger ones there were idiots. This one was quite young, maybe a few years older than I was, but he showed me that he was one of the minority of decent policemen in Norwich. Of course, they let me go soon afterwards, since there was no point in keeping me any longer.

The nearest I ever came to receiving a custodial sentence was in 2001 when I was called to Norwich Magistrates' Court to answer charges of assault. The attack allegedly took place at a Norwich nightclub.

If you read what the press had to say about it at the

time, you could be forgiven for thinking that I go out in the evening to look for trouble. It's not always like that though. In this case, somebody else was looking for it and just happened to drag me along for the ride.

When I am in Norwich, a lot of my African friends come to visit me at my house in Bawburgh. As I have already said, I don't tend to have a lot of people visiting me at home, but around this period it was like the Nigerian High Commission there with people coming and going all the time. A friend called Tim had been spending a lot of time with me in early part of 2000. A few us went to the Ikon nightclub in Norwich for a relaxing evening and everything was fine until Tim started to get edgy. He had seen a man called Ray Boateng who he had some issue with and pretty soon Ray had seen us. He was with a group of people himself. They were all black, so I guess they were African, like him. They kept themselves to themselves. Obviously, they had seen me so they certainly didn't want any trouble.

I told Tim to calm down, that he wasn't doing himself any favours by getting upset in here, but he didn't want to listen. He wandered off towards the group, looking for this guy. I followed him because I wanted to make sure that he wouldn't get himself into any problems. As Tim approached, Boateng separated from the rest of the group and made his way to the dance floor. When I got close enough I heard Boateng and Tim exchange words. As far as I am concerned, that is all that happened before Boateng left.

My friends from Norwich police arrested me that same evening. I thought that I had been invited to the station to help them with their inquiries, but that wasn't the case.

Boateng had reported both of us for assault. He said I had punched him three times, an allegation I hotly disputed. He also claimed that he suffered tenderness at the back of the head. When something like that happens inside a crowded nightclub, there are always dozens of people watching and they all know what happened. Just because I happened to be there, it doesn't mean that I was at fault. It's different with the Crown Prosecution Service, who tend to judge a case on its merits and decide beforehand whether there is sufficient reliable evidence to bring somebody to trial.

A magistrate heard the case at Norwich Magistrates' Court in January 2001. There were witnesses who testified about what had happened but that made no difference. He found me guilty and told me that I could expect to be sent to prison when I returned for sentencing a few weeks later. In that time, a probation officer was asked to file a report on what would be the best form of punishment. There were several options open to the judge, but the probation officer felt that community service would be the most fitting punishment.

The judge decided not to act on his advice and instead sentenced me to house arrest. The probation officer had been against house arrest because he believed it was no punishment at all to lock somebody in a luxury house with a snooker table and swimming pool. I rarely left the house in the daytime anyway, so what difference would it make?

The terms of my house arrest were that I would remain indoors every day for a period of four months between 11am and one 1pm, and then again between 6pm and 2am. I was also required to wear an electronic tagging device around my ankle so that the courts could monitor my movements.

That judge may have thought I would be too afraid to appeal, but I am a proud man and I wasn't prepared to accept a conviction when I hadn't committed a crime. We took the appeal to Norwich Crown Court and Judge David Mellor listened to all the evidence before quashing the conviction. He said that the Boateng's testimony fell a long way short of that needed to secure a conviction.

It was a disgrace the case ever even made it into a courtroom, never mind that it led to a conviction. Thankfully, after all that unnecessary bother, I was able to find a decent judge and clear my name. As a celebrity you sometimes have to be wary because there are a lot of sharks out there. I am glad that I stood up for my rights in this instance. People need to understand that I was made to look like a thug who goes out looking for trouble. Yes, I can be aggressive when I'm provoked – that's my nature – but I am really just a quiet man who wants to be left in peace. I may not be a pacifist, but nor am I a hooligan.

Chapter 14

People are Dogs

When I joined forces with my old mate Jess Harding in 2001, it was the right move for both of us. Two years after my loss to Klitschko I wanted to get back into boxing, and Jess, who had long since retired as a fighter and was now involved in the promotional side of the sport, made me an offer. He was enjoying a successful spell promoting Robin Reid, the former WBC super-middleweight champion, and had Audley Harrison, who the previous year had won a gold medal at the Sydney Olympics and was now beginning his professional career, also signed to his stable. Robin was an experienced man whom Jess couldn't ask to box every week, and Audley was still fighting six-rounders, so he was looking for a well-known boxer who could box on his shows and help him to sell them to the BBC. Colin McMillan knew that I wanted to return, and Jess felt that my name fitted the bill perfectly.

Perhaps I could have made more money elsewhere but,

with Jess having the contract with the BBC, it gave me the opportunity to fight on live television and get myself back in the spotlight, starting with an easy win in Liverpool over a Russian fighter called Alexei Osokin. I sent him to the canvas four times before the fight was stopped in the third round. Graham Everett was again with me as my trainer and I felt so at ease, as if I had never been away.

My fight against Joseph Chingangu, a journeyman boxer from Zambia, which took place two months later, should have been nothing more than a tune-up. While Chingangu was a step up in quality from Osokin, this was still a fight I should have won easily, but it didn't turn out that way.

Things started going wrong for me on the journey up to Newcastle, when my driver crashed the Bentley. The car spun around and it could have been quite nasty but, fortunately for us, we both escaped unhurt.

After that we got lost on the way to the weigh-in. Stories circulated in the press that I had disappeared into the Metro Centre in Gateshead to do some shopping, but that wasn't the case at all. We just had trouble finding the venue and turned up late.

The whole promotion was turning into one big headache for Jess, who had been having enough of his own problems with Chingangu. He was unable to get the permit he needed to enter the UK at first, meaning that he had to return to France until the paperwork could be sorted out. Jess had his work cut out just to make sure that we both got as far as the ring.

On the evening of the fight, at the Telewest Arena, disaster struck. They say that you should protect yourself at all times but there is very little you can do if you get caught with a good shot. After about two minutes of the first round the referee, John Coyle, told us to break. Chingangu hit me with a hard left hook and I went down.

From that moment on I was finished. I would have liked a bit of time to recover from the knockdown but the referee waved the fight on and I was forced to continue. Chingangu floored me twice more before the end of the round.

I'm a fighter and my instinct tells me to continue hitting back, even if it does look like a lost cause. It was no different from the fight with Riddick Bowe in that respect, except for the fact that Chingangu was nowhere near world-championship level. All that goes through your mind when something like that happens is that you have to punch back and get the fight under control again.

I pulled a muscle in my back in the first round, not that it mattered. That first knockdown had taken everything from me. I was fighting on empty from then on and in the second round I was an easy target for Chingangu. He put me down twice more, catching me on both occasions with his right hand. After the second knockdown, which finished the fight, I remained on the canvas for a few minutes while the medical team checked me over. It was my third professional loss, but one that should never have happened. That's boxing though! It was Chingangu's lucky night.

John Hornewer spoke to me after the fight. After I'd beaten Tony Tucker, John had given Brendan Ingle a £5,000 bonus. Jimmy had complained because he was the one who had overseen most of the training and Brendan

175

had been brought in on the night only to help in the corner. I just accepted it – I assumed that John knew what he was doing. Now he made it clear to me why he had done it. 'The only reason you got that fight against Tucker is because Brendan Ingle stood up for you,' he told me. 'When you fought Michael Murray in Manchester and you hit him while he was down, you were lucky not to be disqualified. Brendan was the one who got in the referee's face and made it impossible for him to throw you out. He saw that you were in danger of being thrown out and he knew what to do to save the fight.'

John was right. If I hadn't beaten Murray, I would have been nowhere. Brendan deserved that bonus. But if Brendan had done that for me in the Murray fight, it prompted some questions. Where had my trainer been in this fight? Where was Graham when I was illegally floored by Chingangu? Why didn't he get up on the ring apron and start yelling at the referee? Brendan would have been much more assertive, even aggressive, in creating a fuss and buying me some valuable time to recover. Perhaps I would have lost anyway, but if Graham had been able to buy me some extra time, it would have helped.

It was a devastating loss, but an old friend of mine from Norwich called Dawn Noel made me realise that I had nothing to be ashamed of. Dawn is a clever girl who now works as a solicitor. She has supported me through thick and thin and afterwards she told me, 'Don't worry. Look at your family. Look at your house. That's what you've achieved through boxing and nobody can take that away from you. You've beaten the system.'

I took another hiatus from boxing after that fight.

People are Dogs

Among other things, I wanted to spend some time in Nigeria. There were things I wanted to do there such as build a house and revisit my roots. As a child I had certain friends in our village which I had left behind when I moved to England. After Alan's death I made the journey back to Owerri to visit some of them. There was a boy in the village called Victor Ademola I used to play with as a youngster. He was one of five brothers and I had known all of them.

When I returned for the first time in 2000 Victor was dying of tuberculosis. The news had a real impact on me. I was still coming to terms with Alan's death and now I was confronted with a childhood friend who would also die if he didn't receive the treatment he desperately needed. Tuberculosis can be treated with antibiotics, although this takes several months. It wasn't expensive and I was willing to give his family the money for the medication. It wouldn't have been more than £100 which was easy enough for me to find. I wanted to give his older brother, Benedict, the money but my mother was uncomfortable with it. She told that his compound had been cursed by the devil. Instead, she said, Benedict should come to us so that the elders could hand over the money to him.

Our elders didn't want to know at first. They were afraid and didn't want to deal with Benedict so I told them that I was going to go over there and give him the money myself. Having spent much of my life in England I was a bit less superstitious and I wasn't going to let my friend die for the want of a few pounds just because of a curse. After I had made myself clear the elders agreed to see him and give him the money.

Nothing But Trouble

A letter arrived at my house in Bawburgh several weeks later, long after I had returned to England. It was from Victor, thanking me for all I had done for him and for giving him his life back. For me it had only been a few pounds, but for him it was the difference between life and death. On my next trip to Nigeria, while I was staying in a hotel in Lagos, I heard that Victor was sick again. A friend of mine called Ifeanyi, who knew the Ademola brothers, told me. He said that Benedict hadn't paid for the complete course of medication, that he had kept some of the money for himself. Those drugs weren't expensive, but the treatment took several months and needed to be completed in order for it to be successful.

I was so angry and disappointed. How on earth could Benedict have taken that money when he could see how ill Victor was. All I could think of was how sick Victor had been when I had seen him. His eyes had been as big as apples and he had a terrible, painful cough. It was frightening just to look at him.

Ifeanyi had told me then that if I wanted to help Victor then I shouldn't give any more money to his family. The only way I could be sure he received the treatment was by taking him to the hospital myself. People in the village had told me not to go near him, that I would catch the illness myself. Of course, living in England as a teenager I had already been inoculated against tuberculosis so his illness posed no risk to me, but the villagers weren't to know that.

Here I was, the heavyweight champion for the world, lying on my bed in the Sheraton Hotel in Lagos, crying my eyes out about my dying friend. How was I to help him from here? I decided that the best thing to do

People are Dogs

would be to bring Victor to Lagos. That way I could take him to the hospital myself, pay the doctors myself, and watch over him to make sure that he was getting the correct treatment.

I asked Ifeanyi if he would go back to Owerri and bring Victor to me. He said he couldn't, but that Victor's older brother who lived here in Lagos, Emanuel, would be able to do it. Emanuel looked just like Victor. I told him that I wouldn't give him the money directly, but that I would pay for the flights to get him and Victor to Owerri and that when they were here I would pay for the treatment. After that we never saw him again.

What could I say about this? I had spent months watching my own brother die and I would have done anything to help him. These guys had the chance to save Victor very easily. It wasn't going to cost them anything, but they still thought only of themselves. It made me sick. I just couldn't understand how they could act like that. The head of the family, another brother called Sunday, came to visit me at the hotel. He wanted to speak on Emanuel's behalf.

'It's not as bad as it seems,' he told me, trying to defend Emanuel's actions.

'How can you say that?' I asked him. Victor was in danger of dying and all Sunday seemed worried about was protecting the good name of the family. 'Your brother is going to die and you come here and tell me that things aren't all that bad. Get out of my hotel, you bastard!'

A couple of weeks later Victor passed away. It was so senseless. We could have saved his life so easily. I tried to do everything for him but, with so many people who were only interested in their own welfare, he didn't stand a chance. It's something I will never understand.

There was another, younger, brother in the family called Ojembe. He had had nothing to do with Victor's death as far as I was concerned. He was the youngest of the family, around my age, and I felt sorry for him because I imagined he felt the same sense of loss for Victor as I did for Alan. Later on he decided that he would move to England and as he knew me he chose Norwich as his new home. I was in Nigeria when he left and I can remember the party we had for him before his journey. His mother was so happy for him. She kept telling me that I should look out for him once I was back.

When he reached England he had all sorts of problems. His visa wasn't correct and he had to apply for asylum. I arranged a lawyer for him so that he had a better chance of staying in the country. Even the lawyer thought that he should return to Nigeria after a time, that it was hopeless trying to get him asylum. I carried on fighting for him, even when nobody else would. For me it was a matter of honour, of keeping my word to his mother.

After that he disappeared and changed his name. He wanted the good life but he didn't want me any longer – I had fulfilled my purpose for him. That's how some people are. They will use you when they need you and forget about you when they don't. They are just dogs. Ojembe, it turned out, was no better than the rest of his family.

Part of it may be down to the fat white girl he took up with. He was a good-looking guy, too good for her, and she knew that if he carried on hanging around with me he was likely to find somebody better. By keeping him away from me she was protecting herself. It all brought home to me just how cheap and worthless friendship can be for some people.

Chapter 15

'Herbie, Me Got Me Gun . . .'

If you were to believe what some so-called experts say, one of my reasons for leaving England is that I was forced out by certain gangsters. This is a fairly common misconception and, even though it isn't true, I can understand why people may choose to believe it. In Norwich it is common knowledge that I have been associated with some rather unsavoury characters in the past. Coupled with the fact that I have spent a lot of my time in the USA and Germany in recent years, it's quite easy to put two and two together and make five.

There is some truth to the rumour that one or two gangsters helped me to make my decision to leave England behind for a while, though not in the way that people have suggested. While I wanted to get away from those in the gangster scene, it wasn't for fear of what they might do to me. My concern was that I might end up in prison. Trouble often seemed to be lurking around every corner and it wouldn't always be of my making.

Nothing But Trouble

You have only to look at my dealings with the Norwich Yardies to realise that they held no fear for me. Actually, they were the ones who were afraid of what I would do to them. The Yardies are a criminal movement who specialise in the sale of drugs – crack cocaine and marijuana in particular – and are well known for their involvement with illegal firearms. Their members are of West Indian origin and they get their name from the government yards in the most impoverished parts of Kingston, Jamaica. It was there, in the neighbourhood of Trenchtown, that the first gangs were formed. That was in the 1950s and today they have spread from Jamaica to all of the major cities in the United Kingdom – and Norwich is no exception.

One of their number, a guy everybody knew as Prima, used to be a friend of mine. When I first met him he had just arrived in England from Jamaica. We got along well and, seeing that he was an intelligent kind of guy, I agreed to lend him some money so that he could go to college and make a better life for himself. I could afford it and I was happy to be able to help him out.

As I found out later, he didn't use the money for his education at all. Instead he invested it in drugs and became quite successful at what he was doing. I remember arriving back in England in May 2002 after a family holiday in Portugal, when I first heard about his activities from my friend Courtney. He said, 'You see Prima? You know what he's doing now? He's selling drugs.'

'What?' I asked him. I couldn't believe what I was hearing.

'Yeah,' he said. 'That money you gave him, he used it

184

for crack and to bring girls from Jamaica. You need to get away from this because the police will want to bring you into it if they can.'

He was right and I had to consider my next move very carefully. I clearly needed to dissociate myself from him as quickly as possible. Drugs have never been my scene and I certainly didn't want to be friends with somebody who was involved with them on that level. On the other hand, I hadn't forgotten the loan.

It was a Friday afternoon when I called him. 'Prima,' I said, 'I want my money back.'

He answered in his Jamaican drawl, 'Herbie, me got me gun now.'

'You got your what?'

'Yeah, man,' he said, this time slower so that I could make no mistake, 'me got me gun.'

I said, 'What do you think? That I sold my one?' There were two options: either be a man and get my money back or be a coward and write it off. I put down the phone down and went looking for him with my friend Courtney.

No matter how big he now thought he was in the underworld, nobody was going to threaten me and get away with it. I fight for my money – not just in the ring but in life as well. He didn't frighten me because I am afraid of nobody. Did he really think that, by mentioning his gun, he would make me run away? Not a bit of it. I have a gun myself, albeit a legally owned one. My house is set in several acres of land and I am licensed to shoot rabbits on the property.

We didn't know where he was living, but Courtney had heard about a crack den that he had set up from where he could supply the drugs. When we arrived at the place there were junkies all over the place, most of them on the floor. A slim Jamaican girl met us at the door. She was clearly one of the women Prima had been bringing into the country to work for him. As it turns out, Prima had plenty more of her kind working for him – he must have thought he was Scarface. I asked her, 'Where's Prima?'

She went into one of the rooms and when she came back she had wet herself. Although I had heard the saying about people wetting themselves when they were afraid, I never knew that it could actually happen. This girl just lost control of her bladder.

'Where's Prima?' I asked her again.

'Hold on, hold on!' she said. 'Me call him now.' She phoned him and found out that he was at home.

Prima's driver, a Londoner called Dave, took us over there. The girl came with us too. When we arrived, the girl got out of the car and ran away. Dave waited in the car for us.

There were four people in the house. Prima was there with his girlfriend, a fellow Yardie known as Shotman, and Shotman's girlfriend. It was Prima's girl who opened the door, although only enough to peer out and see who was there. At that point I barged my way in.

The first thing I saw was Shotman walking down the stairs. He quickly turned around and ran back up before jumping straight through a window. I ran after him to see what had happened. Broken glass was everywhere and his leg was badly damaged. As I looked out of the window I saw him crawling away.

I shouted down to where Prima was sitting, 'I want my money, Prima.'

'Herbie, Me Got Me Gun . . .'

'I'll go and get your money, Herbie,' he said. Courtney was supposed to be keeping an eye on him but he escaped through the open door and into the street.

Shotman's girlfriend was still upstairs. I guess she must have been terrified because she, too, tried to escape through the window – the one Shotman had used. She was, though – to put it nicely – a very big Jamaican girl and she got stuck in the window frame. Courtney and I just looked at each other – we had lost two gangsters and now we had a candidate for the Butterfly Lounge trapped by her own girth right in front of us. She became hysterical, screaming blue murder in her West Indian dialect and sweating like a pig. Her feet were kicking out behind her and this just meant that she became wedged in even further. It was one of the funniest things I have ever seen and both of us started laughing. We couldn't leave her like that though, so we pulled her back onto the floor. She was a shivering wreck, so we left her to her own devices on the carpet.

Prima's girl came with us in the car as we went looking for him.

Once Prima realised that his girlfriend hadn't escaped with him he became worried. My mobile rang and he started pleading with me. 'Herbie, bring me girl back. Herbie, bring me girl back.'

After that he called the police. That's what kind of gangster he was – first he ran away from us, leaving his girlfriend to fend for herself, and then he brings in the Old Bill. We couldn't believe it when we found out what had happened. He told them that we had abducted her at gunpoint and that we were trying to kill him.

We heard it first on the car radio. The girl agreed to

come with us, so it wasn't kidnap. Even so, at this point we decided that it would be better to offload her, so we let her out somewhere in Norwich.

When he called back again, and I told him that I still wanted my money, he said, 'OK, Herbie, you can keep the girl.'

Before long the city was crawling with police and we needed to get off the streets before we were arrested. Dave dropped me off at my friend Ken's place, where I was able to lie low for a few hours in the hope that all of this would die down.

It didn't take too long before both Courtney and Dave were arrested. This was despite the fact that Dave had only taken us in his car. He had done nothing, so there was no need to arrest him. Thankfully, he refused to help the police in their investigations against us.

During the night the police had raided my house. After hearing from Prima that I was rampaging around Norwich brandishing a gun they were clearly concerned about the welfare of my family. As it was, Helen and Henry were not at home. It was a real blessing, because a group of armed officers storming our home might have frightened them to death. The police in Norwich can be horrible, so I guess they would have taken great delight in this unannounced visit.

Before I arrived at his house, Ken had seen the reports on television that I was running amok through Norwich and he still helped me out. For me, that was a demonstration of real character and true loyalty. On Saturday morning I told him that I wanted to go home, which wasn't at all easy with the police attempting to catch me by blocking the streets.

'Herbie, Me Got Me Gun . . .'

Ken doesn't have any legs so he is confined to a wheelchair. However, he can still drive, since he has a car that has been specially adapted for his disability and allows him to control everything with his hands. This gave me the opportunity to use the space below the steering wheel, where the pedals are in a regular car, as a hiding place. The police were searching cars and when they stopped Ken my chest was thumping. I thought I was going to have a heart attack but they didn't look in the place where his legs would normally have been and allowed us to continue.

As we approached the house I could see that the police were still searching it. Two officers were guarding the front of the building, which meant that there was no chance of our getting past them unseen.

We drove towards the back of the property and Ken dropped me there. I knew that when the police had finished whatever it was they were doing inside the house, they wouldn't be back, so all I needed to do was wait for a while. Once evening arrived I decided to make a move.

From my position at the rear of the property it was a long way to the house. Walking would have been too dangerous because the police were still looking for me, so I grabbed one of my horses and rode him back. It was a lot quicker than walking but he was unsaddled so I had to hang on to his mane. By the time I climbed off his back, covering the last short distance to the house on my hands and knees, my bum was really sore.

Even though the house was locked I was still able to get inside fairly easily. Then I had a long hot bath before changing into some fresh clothes and making myself something to eat.

Nothing But Trouble

By now you are probably wondering why I went home in the first place. What was I thinking of, going back to the house when I could have gone into hiding somewhere other than Norwich? Well, I knew that the situation was getting serious and I didn't want to become a fugitive. It was quite clear to me that I couldn't stay on the run for very long and that I would have to talk to the police sooner or later. The problem was it was Saturday and, if the police had caught me, they would have kept me in a cell over the weekend. Only the magistrates' court can grant bail and, since they were not open, the police would have had no option other than to detain me until the beginning of the working week. My house was considerably more comfortable than a police station so it made sense for me to stay there instead.

The police had no idea where I was. They were searching everywhere for me. Everywhere, that is, except for the one place where I was hiding. The funny thing was that, while they were guarding the house, I was able to watch them on my video surveillance system. They spent the whole weekend looking for me and I could see them the whole time.

I kept myself awake for two days. Although I was sure that the police would not come back inside the house, I wanted to be on my guard the whole time. If they came back, I wanted to know that they were in the house before *they* knew that *I* was.

It was about five o'clock on the Monday morning when I decided the time was right to surrender. A policemen was still guarding the front door so I pressed the intercom and said, 'Hello.'

'Yeah, who is it?' he asked. He was completely taken aback because they had had no idea that anybody was in the house.

'You're looking for Herbie Hide, aren't you?' I said.

'Is that you, Herbie?'

'Yeah.'

His next move surprised me. He got into the police car and drove off at high speed. At first I thought perhaps they didn't want me after all but later I realised that he was following orders from his superiors. He had been there only to watch over the house while they thought I was away. Once it dawned on them that I was inside, they were afraid that I would start shooting at them from the windows.

Five or ten minutes later, the police were back. By then I had changed into my best suit – I wanted to be dressed appropriately for the magistrate – and I went outside. Several armed officers rushed at me but I remained calm. 'What's happening, guys?' I said. 'Time to make a move. Let's go!'

I wasn't really worried because I knew that the police were far more interested in Prima than they were in me, or at least he was a higher priority than I was. They had had him under surveillance for a while and now they had the opportunity to catch him.

Even so, my name carries a fair amount of credibility as far as the Norfolk police are concerned. Their theory, as I understand it – and you can judge for yourself – is that I had a sawn-off gun with me when I went looking for Prima.

Then there was a young junkie at the den who also suffered bullet wounds, this time to his stomach. He reported this to the police, and they even took photos of the injuries, but he never returned to the station.

They also claimed that a hardened gangster like Prima would not have jumped through a window just because I was looking a bit upset. The same goes for Shotman, although clearly they could not vouch for the mindset of the obese lady. There were bullet marks on the stair rail, but who was to say that I had caused them?

Had these charges stuck, I might have been facing a good few years at Her Majesty's pleasure, but the police had no way of proving them. By the time they finally caught up with me it was Monday morning, two and a half days after the alleged shootings. They may have found firearms in the house – no crime there, since they were licensed – but I would have had ample time to dispose of a gun had it been a sawn-off. Furthermore, I had washed and changed my clothes since then, so there was absolutely no possibility of their finding gunpowder residue on my person. Even so, the magistrate still decided to remand Courtney and me in custody for a week on suspicion of abducting Prima's girl at gunpoint, and we were sent to Norwich prison.

We all have our notions of what life in jail must be like. Strangely enough, I wasn't at all frightened at the prospect. The prison in Norwich is a relatively small facility, catering mostly for remand prisoners and small-time crooks. When I arrived there, delivered in one of those large prison vans, I was surprised to hear inmates hollering my name from the windows. All I could hear was, 'Herbie! Herbie!' and I wondered how the hell they knew I was coming. To my knowledge, prison was a place where you were locked up in a cell with no access to the outside world. It was only later that I realised that they had televisions and radios in there – everything they would need to keep them up to date with my recent adventures.

As I was led to my cell, one that I would be sharing with Courtney, the other prisoners were offering me things. They wanted to know if I needed shampoo, or towels, or chocolate. I didn't want any of these things from them so I refused. It was my first day in the place and I had no idea how important these small luxuries were in prison. I mistakenly thought that stuff like this would be supplied as and when I needed it.

I was quite happy to be sharing a cell with Courtney. We spent the first day telling each other stories, Courtney's about Jamaica and mine about Nigeria. Under the circumstances we were having quite a relaxed time, but that changed during the evening when a group of screws turned up at our cell and asked me to step outside. I felt threatened by this and immediately turned defensive. 'Get back from me,' I said, 'or I'll beat up all of you fuckers.'

They didn't try anything, they just told me to come with them. The place they took me to was awful. It was the wing of the prison reserved for the high-risk inmates. Every prisoner has his own cell and from there you cannot see anybody. I spent four or five hours lying on my bed listening to what was going on. The whole time I could hear people making a noise, trying to speak to whoever could hear them. They would shout, 'Are you listening?' to nobody in particular in the hope that somebody would answer.

I hadn't caused any trouble on the main landing, so

there was no explanation for moving me to this part of the prison. I shouted out to see if anybody could help me, 'Are you listening?'

'Yeah, I'm listening,' somebody shouted back.

'Why am I here?' I explained to him why I was in the prison in the first place.

'That ain't nothin',' he said, after listening to what I had been remanded for. 'You shouldn't really be here.'

Then somebody else piped up, 'Are you listening?'

'Yeah,' the first guy answered him.

'I think he's that Herbie Hide.'

'Yeah, it's me,' I said. 'What have they put me here for?'

'Because they don't want people walking around on the landing with a broken jaw,' he told me. In other words, the screws knew that I could cause trouble and they wanted to show me who was stronger. I asked him why he was in the nick and he told me about the armed robbery he never carried out and the person he never killed – everybody is innocent in prison, especially the guilty ones.

The place was horrible and I wanted to get out. You couldn't see anybody, you didn't know what time of day it was and, if you needed to go to the bathroom, a screw had to escort you. I wanted to get back to the landing where I had been before they collected me. 'I don't feel well,' I told my neighbour.

'Nobody feels well in here. I've been here for seven years and I've never felt well.'

'I'm feeling sick. I need to go to hospital.'

He started laughing. 'You need to go to hospital? Wait until next week when you get to see the doctor.'

'What if I really am ill?' I asked him. 'What then?'

'I'll tell you what to do,' he said. 'Look behind you. Do you see that radiator pipe? Put your arm in there.' I did as he asked me. 'Now snap your arm!'

'Fuck off!' I told him.

'Well, I was only trying to help,' he said.

The next morning a prison service official came to assess me. He said that there was no need for me to be held in this part of the prison any longer, and I was moved back to the landing. I felt much happier after this because it meant that I was with Courtney again.

Being in a prison environment isn't an ideal situation for anybody, and for a celebrity it can be even more daunting. On the outside I am famous for my fighting abilities, so there was always the possibility that some hard case would want to try his luck against me. As I have already said, the prison didn't frighten me as such, but I was aware that I needed to be on my guard and, if there was even a hint of trouble, it was to be nipped in the bud. On our landing the inmates were free to come and go from their cells as they pleased during the mealtimes, meaning that everybody had access to me. Then it happened: I was at the pool table when somebody shouted out, 'Herbie, you fucking kerb crawler.'

I looked around and several people were standing around at the doors of their cells. 'Who said that?'

Nobody answered. It could have been any one of them, but I wasn't about to let this lie. 'OK,' I said. 'Either the big guy who said it owns up now or I'm going to come over there and beat up every single one of you.'

Just like that, everybody pointed directly at one person.

Nothing But Trouble

He was a little skinny guy who looked as if he had just crapped himself. I glared at him, flaring my nostrils, but I decided not to do anything to him. I probably would have snapped his back just by grabbing him. It did the trick because the next day a group of prisoners approached Courtney and me to ask permission to beat up a guard. Suddenly we were the top dogs on the landing and people would do as we said. I would have been quite happy to let them attack a screw – what did he matter to me? – but Courtney is a bit more level headed and he told them not to.

You had to do everything for yourself inside those walls. When I was at boarding school we would go into the canteen, put our food on a plate and give the plate back when we had finished. There were people there to do that kind of work. In prison you had your own plate and cutlery and once you had finished eating you could wash them in a little sink. It was so dirty, it's a wonder people weren't catching diseases.

Something that really struck me about the prison system is that it doesn't work. Don't get me wrong, I know that jails are there to punish the bad guys, and that's fine. It's their other function – the part where criminals are rehabilitated so that they can be reintroduced to perform a useful role in society – that is lost on me. In my experience, a jail is a training ground for villains. Nowhere else would you get so many lawbreakers under one roof, swapping stories, each trying to prove himself the top man in the joint. Much of what a criminal knows on the outside has been learnt on the inside.

What really annoyed me during my stay was the fact

that Prima, a real criminal and a danger to society, was still at large, while Courtney and I were locked up like animals. It was a ridiculous situation. They knew exactly what Prima was doing and they had him under surveillance. He could have been brought in at any time but, once they did that, the kidnapping case against us would be doomed. And while this was going on, Prima was trying to supply the police with more evidence against us in the form of testimonies.

Thankfully my solicitor, Simon Nicholls, was able to show the judge what a flimsy case the prosecution had when we reappeared in court at the end of the week. The judge released us and the charges against Courtney and me were finally dropped six weeks later.

The police were still watching me though. The day I arrived home I spent some time relaxing alone by the pond. As I was feeding my coy carp, lost in my own thoughts, I heard Helen shout at me from an upstairs window. She was pointing at the sky, where a police helicopter was hovering. There was nothing more for them to see though.

Funnily enough, I met Shotman sometime later. There were no hard feelings on my part as my grievance had been with Prima. His leg was still in plaster after jumping from the window. He told me that he had been with Prima when he had threatened me on the phone. 'You told Herbie that?' he had said to him.
Prima answered, 'Yeah, why not?'

'It's wrong,' Shotman told him. 'Herbie's not going to bottle. He's not a coward. He won the title at twenty-two years of age, so he isn't going to hide from you. He's going to fight you all the way. He lent you money and all he wants is his money back with no interest. He's your friend and you say, "Me got me gun." You must be crazy.'

He said that he had known that I would find them and he had wanted to leave, but that Prima didn't believe I would come.

I'm still waiting for Prima to give me my money back, but I don't think he's in any hurry to start the repayments. Maybe I should start charging him interest. It wasn't really about the money though. It was about showing people that I stand up for my principles. Whatever they say now about my reasons for leaving the United Kingdom, nobody can say that it's because I am afraid of gangsters.

Chapter 16

Gangster Shit

It was time for me to leave England. I needed to get my boxing career back on track, return to the gym and start fighting again. After the fight with Chingangu I bought a house in Las Vegas, and once all the nonsense with Prima had died down I decided it would be best to move over there and rebuild my life.

There was no real plan in place when I arrived in America. I didn't have a trainer or promoter, so it was like starting from scratch. I joined the Nevada Partners gym in the north of Las Vegas and trained there by myself. It didn't take long before I met a whole host of new faces.

One of the first people I came across at Nevada Partners was Steve 'Crocodile' Fitch, Mike Tyson's former motivator. Crocodile is one of those guys who hang around the gyms in Las Vegas. Mike Tyson had heard that I was training in Vegas and he dropped by at the gym to pay me a visit. Mike's the biggest superstar in the sport but he's also the type of person who knows about everybody in boxing.

Anyway, when he called I wasn't there. I just heard from the other guys in the gym that he had been asking after me. The thing that bothered me was that he may have been wanting to use me as a sparring partner, but I couldn't ask him if that was the case because I hadn't seen him. That's how I got to know Crocodile. I asked him what Mike wanted from me. He said, 'Nothing, man. Mike knows you're here and he just wants to hang with you.' I didn't know what he meant by 'hang'. It sounded a bit gay to me, but it wasn't.

I got to know Crocodile very well and he played an important role in my team. He was always there for me, making sure that I woke up at the right time, fixing my coffee for me before I left the house and ensuring that I went for my run. Mike would drive by and pick him up from the house, but he would never come in.

The Nevada Partners gym was the place where I got talking to Eddie Mustafa Muhammad. Mustafa had been a world-class fighter himself, holding the WBA light-heavyweight title for a while in the early 1980s, but I knew him as a trainer. He had been in Michael Bentt's corner when we met for the championship in 1994 and I hadn't liked him at all. I thought he had been disrespectful of me by telling everybody that Michael was going to beat me easily. That was in the past though, and when we got talking he agreed that he would train me, together with Mike McCallum.

Mustafa was an excellent trainer – one the best I have ever worked with. What I really liked about him was his manner during a fight when he was standing in my corner. He was just so calm and collected. Whatever was happening in the fight, he knew how to settle me. I didn't have to worry about anything. If something was going wrong, Mustafa would reassure me that the fight was over 12 rounds and that we had plenty of time to put it right. If Mustafa had been in my corner for the Klitschko fight, I am sure he would have helped me to win. He would have seen that something wasn't right after the first round and acted accordingly.

In the gym Mustafa didn't take any nonsense from anybody and could be pretty loud. Mike McCallum, on the other hand, was always quiet. They had been friends for a long time and they complemented each other as trainers. Together they made a terrific team.

Another thing I appreciated about Mustafa was that he was extremely loyal to his fighters. He wasn't afraid of anybody and that's probably why he was able to help them. Mustafa would keep an eye on his boxers, whatever problems they may have been having in their lives away from boxing. He's worked with people such as James Toney and Johnny Tapia, people who are notorious for being difficult to deal with, so he was just the kind of person I needed in my corner.

Mustafa was also very demanding. He once wanted me to spar with Kelvin Davis, the former IBF cruiserweight champion. I told him that I was fatigued, but it was no good. Mustafa had organised the sparring session with Kelvin's brother and he didn't want me to pull out, even though I hadn't agreed to it in the first place. Mustafa said to me, 'The fatigue will go out the window. Just watch, this guy will come at you like a train. It will be good for you.' I agreed to do a couple of rounds just to keep him happy.

Kelvin, who had a tattoo on his face well before Mike Tyson copied the idea, couldn't touch me in there. At the same time, I was too tired to put any effort into hurting him and after the third round I had had enough and wanted to end the session. His brother thought otherwise and insisted that we continue for another round. In the fourth round I gave him a beating.

He came back to spar with me again the next day, and this time I was in the mood for some real sparring with him. I ran circles around him in the first round and then, just after the second round had started, I jabbed him with the left and then blasted him with a right to the chin. He was out cold. The brother, who was already a bit of a loudmouth, jumped in the ring and started attacking me. Mustafa was in there like a flash to pull him off.

Kelvin never really did anything much after that and was lucky to survive a training accident in which he had to jump from a bridge to avoid an oncoming truck in New Zealand.

Something similar happened with another fighter, Cliff Couser. I sparred with him at the Top Rank Gym and, as is usually the case with my sparring partners, I beat the stuffing out of him. Mustafa called a halt to the session when he saw that Couser was getting hurt, and I turned around to leave the ring. That was when he body-slammed me. I felt my feet leaving the floor and the next thing I knew Couser had bent my leg behind my back.

Again, as with Kelvin Davis's brother, Mustafa pulled him off very quickly. Then I heard Richard Steel, who owned the gym, shouting that somebody should stop

Couser leaving. He wanted to get to his car but nobody in the gym wanted to let him get that far. You get to meet some very funny people in American gyms.

I still didn't have a promoter after Jess Harding and I had gone our separate ways following the Chingangu fight, but that was to change after the boxing writer Steve Bunce visited me at my home for a television interview. He told me about a new kid on the block who was making some waves in the UK. His name was Mick Hennessy and after I called him we agreed that we could do some business together. I would live and train in Las Vegas and then travel over to England for my fights. That way I would have the best of both worlds – the best available preparation over in the US and then appearances on British shows where my name was much better known.

Derek McCafferty was booked as my first opponent, scheduled for eight rounds at the Ice Arena in Nottingham in April 2003. Our fight was on the undercard, with Howard Eastman fighting against Scott Dann in the main event.

Graham Everett called me. It had been a while since we had spoken and he said that he would like to come to the fight in Nottingham. I told him that I would be happy to have him there as a guest and that I would sort it out with Mickey.

Mustafa was with me at my home in Bawburgh when I found out about the hotel-room allocation. Four rooms had been booked, one each for Mustafa, Mike, Mickey and me. I called Mickey's assistant, Debbie, immediately and told her that if they didn't organise a room for Graham, they could forget the whole show. After I finished, Mustafa said to me, 'Are you serious? Mickey flew us over here business class. He's paying us to fight. And you tell him to go fuck himself over a hotel room? Man, this guy must be a true friend of yours.'

He was right. Graham was a friend and I was determined to keep my word. We go back a long way together. He was one of the first people to take an interest in me when I joined the Lads' Club and for that I will always be grateful.

He had always been around the sport. His father was a trainer and would coach Graham when he was active as a fighter. Boxing was everything to him and later, when he was working as a trainer himself at the Lads' Club, he was seen as a sensible head offering sound advice. I always looked up to him as a youngster. One of the nicest things I ever heard him say was, 'When Norwich City get to the Cup final and Herbie Hide wins the ABAs, that will make my year.' That really touched me – I felt elated that he could think like that about me. It was the point when I began to think of him as a close friend.

After that I always felt that he was there for me. He would come to all of my fights and would never have a bad word said about me.

As I moved to Matchroom it was also an opportunity for Graham to improve his own prospects. He became friendly with Freddie King to the point where, if there was a problem in the gym, or some kind of conflict where I was involved, Freddie would speak to Graham rather than approach me directly. Invariably, it seemed to me that Graham would take the side of Freddie, or whichever other person from Matchroom was involved.

I had the feeling that he didn't want to upset anybody in Romford.

Towards the end of my time at Matchroom, Graham had got his professional trainer's licence. He had a couple of lads who would appear on some of the Matchroom shows, but the fights dried up after I left. Without me his days there were numbered.

During my time at Wincobank, when I was training for my comeback against Michael Murray under Brendan Ingle, I called Graham and asked him to join me in Sheffield. I was getting bored there and wanted to have somebody from the old days to keep me company. He joined me there two weeks before the fight, acting as Brendan's number two.

A trainer needs to be careful whom he employs as his second-in-command. Even the best trainers out there, and Brendan Ingle certainly belongs in that category, can lose their fighter. It doesn't matter how talented the trainer is, if the second is a good talker and can get inside the head of the boxer, the trainer will lose his fighter.

For the next fight Graham was my trainer, Brendan wasn't. It was only for one fight though, because when Frank Warren organised the title fight against Tucker he wanted Jimmy.

When I went after Prima it was partly because I felt rejected by Graham. I had been trying to call him from Portugal before I arrived back in England. It was May 2002, a few months after I had lost to Chingangu, and I wanted to get back in the gym. But I wasn't able to contact Graham.

Something similar happened when I was taken to court for driving while disqualified two years later. Despite the community service I was ordered to carry out, I still wanted to continue with my training. The only way I could do this was by remaining in Norwich and training with Graham. He said I should train in London instead. This was out of the question. There was no way I could complete my community service in Norwich if I was living in London. At the same time, if I was to stay in Norwich, I wouldn't be able to train. That was why I went back to America, where I could train without any legal obligations. It was short sighted, but I didn't feel I had many other options.

Graham still thought of me as a friend. He told me that what I needed, more than his help, was my family. He thought that Helen could be of much more help to me than he could ever be at this point in my life.

I also have to admit that training me was never an easy job for Graham. Now he is a hugely respected trainer, working at the Kickstop Gym in Norwich with some top-quality fighters on his roster. He has guided Jonathan Thaxton to the British title and continues to look after him today, along with the promising Walsh brothers, Liam, Ryan and Michael, of whom big things are expected. His stock is high at the moment, and he deserves the respect he has earned in boxing, but it wasn't always that way. I was always demanding as a young fighter and Graham would often bear the brunt of my frustrations. Maybe we were both too young for each other in those days. When he called me I was glad to have him back in my life.

You may think that a boxer like Derek McCafferty should cause no problems at all for a fighter like me. He came into the fight having only won 2 of his 16 previous fights so, on paper, it looked as if I should have blown him away. But boxing doesn't always work like that. For all those losses on his record he had built up a wealth of experience, fighting some of the better British heavyweights such as Pele Reid and Michael Sprott, so he knew a thing or two about surviving in the boxing ring. It was another comeback fight for me, after a year and a half away, and I was rusty. McCafferty could take a punch, and when you face a guy like that – somebody with a good chin, who also covers up the whole time and refuses to get hit – it can be very frustrating. I danced around him for the whole fight, beating him up, but it wasn't until the seventh round that I was finally able to get him out of there. All in all, it proved to be a tough fight, but one that gave me a few valuable rounds.

Next up was a chance for revenge. After my loss against Joseph Chingangu in 2001, many people had written me off. Five knockdowns in one fight, including the left hook I felt sure landed after the referee had told us to break, looked bad and I can understand why they may have thought my time had passed. Whatever they believed, I certainly wasn't shot and I wanted the opportunity to put things right. That's why I was delighted when Mickey organised a rematch with Chingangu at the Goresbrook Leisure Centre in Dagenham, the venue where I had beaten Michael Murray for the British title a decade earlier.

That first fight had been a fluke. Chingangu got lucky after that left hook. On any other night I would have battered him and I was determined to prove it this time around. I told everybody that I would win this fight in the first round, and that was exactly what I did.

Nothing But Trouble

Chingangu barely managed a punch while I went to work on him. I knocked him down twice, the first time from a hard right. He beat the count, so I put him down again, this time with a big left hook followed by another right. He made as if he were going to get up but his heart wasn't in it and he let the referee, Ian John-Lewis, count him out.

It's easy enough for me to go around telling everybody that the first fight was a freak result. Thankfully, I was able to back up those words with actions.

Although Mustafa was employed as my head trainer, I was becoming frustrated by the amount of time he was dedicating to other matters. He was involved with a boxers' union and this meant that he needed to be constantly on the move, visiting other cities. All of this impacted on the number of hours he could spend with me in the gym, which certainly wasn't ideal. It got to the stage where I felt that Mustafa was turning up only when I was fighting, and a boxer needs more from his trainer than just a cornerman. This is an exaggeration, but I really needed more input from Mustafa in the gym. For this reason I hired Don House to help with the day-to-day gym activities.

As is the way with trainers after you have worked with them for a while, Don wanted to be seen as the main man. He could certainly see that Mustafa was not a regular in the gym and, rightly or wrongly, he felt that he was doing more of the work while Mustafa was picking up the lion's share of the money. To be honest, I preferred working with Mustafa but I had to think about my career and I couldn't base it on his schedule.

One day I was training at the gym with Don when

Gangster Shit

Mustafa walked in and saw us. Don was working with me in the ring on the pads and, as anybody in boxing will tell you, only the head trainer takes the fighter on the pads. I knew this, Don knew this and Mustafa definitely knew it. He said to Don, 'You better get out of that ring.' Don's not a tough guy and there was no way he was going to argue with Mustafa. But Mustafa is also a guy who has his fighter's interests at heart, as he showed when my life started to get out of control in America.

One of my problems is that I get bored very easily. Helen needed to go back to England so, without her and the kids, I was left by myself. I found myself looking for some entertainment away from the gym and started going to clubs in Las Vegas. It was there that I got to know some gangsters. We got on pretty well and before long I was part of their social scene, going to parties and messing around. They had their guns, but that was nothing new for guys like this in America. Over there you can purchase a firearm almost as easily as you can buy a hamburger. Many people see it as a form of defence.

After the Kulikauskas fight, which I lost due to a bad cut, I really lost interest in the sport. Fighting is what I do, and what I should have been doing, but I was in a world of my own. I had been wild in the past but, for the first time, I was living right on the edge, hanging with my gangster buddies. Maybe I thought I was having fun, that my life away from the boxing ring could offer me much more than the gym ever could.

My attitude stank and my dedication dwindled. I was staying out until all hours and coming into the gym when I felt like it. Many trainers were afraid even to work with me because they could see what I was turning into. I had become impossible.

Some of the people I was messing with were out of control. One guy I was close to was arrested for murder while I was there. We called him Airhorn – everybody had a nickname in the 'hood – and he shot a prostitute called Chocolate, who owed him some money. There was no messing about. She had a debt and he killed her for it. Now he's doing life. I'm told that he was caught because her pimp, a guy called Ice Cream, grassed on him.

Airhorn had already been in trouble a few weeks before. We had met up one evening in a bar and he wanted to take revenge on somebody who had shot one of his friends. He asked me to drive him over there but I didn't want to know. There was no way that I was getting myself involved in a drive-by shooting. In the end Airhorn went off by himself and the police picked him up pretty quickly. When they found his gun it was dirty. By that I mean that it had already been used, and people don't waste bullets in the 'hood.

Without his gun he wasn't as strong as he liked to think he was. One night he brought a stripper back to my house. In Vegas, some of the strippers will sleep with you, but a lot of them won't. This one just took his money and left. He let her leave but he exploded afterwards – he wanted to find her and kill her.

One of the guys in the crew, known to the rest of us as Rock, worked as a pimp himself. I was there when he got into some trouble at the Stratosphere Hotel. This was after he coaxed a girl from Los Angeles away from her own pimp to work for him. She was working up in one of the rooms there and he wanted to check on her, to make sure that she was doing her job correctly, so we all went along with him and waited down in the lobby while he went upstairs to see her.

Pimping is a tough trade, and this guy from Los Angeles was less than impressed with Rock. We didn't know it at the time but the guy had come to Las Vegas to claim his girl back. He had followed us into the Stratosphere and then went to the girl's room to find Rock, leaving him with a bullet in the head. He thought he had killed him, and ran away. Rock survived the shooting, but he was in a bad way when the ambulance came for him. He's a tough fella though, and it didn't take long before he was out earning money again with his ladies of the night. He didn't even bother with painkillers.

It was crazy to be associated with these kinds of people and things started to change only once I realised I was getting in too deep. It all started when a so-called friend of mine, one of the guys I would sometimes hang out with, stole my chequebook. I'm not stupid enough to believe in honour among thieves – my dealings with Prima in Norwich were enough to teach me that there is no code of conduct where people like this are concerned – but I still didn't expect these guys to try stealing my money.

At first I didn't realise that he had taken it. He was writing himself cheques for small amounts – $200 here, $300 there – and the banks were giving him the cash. In America they are much less stringent. As long as you show your ID they will give you the money, and it's no problem to fake an ID. Then he got cheeky and tried to write a cheque for $1 million. There wasn't that much money in the account, so that bank asked me about it. It was then that I knew that somebody had been robbing me, although I didn't know who.

Another friend told me about it. I say he was a friend but I use the term loosely, because the only reason he came to me was out of spite. He was annoyed at not being cut in on the scam and he wanted to get his own back. At first I didn't want to believe it but once I knew it was true my mood changed and I called him up. It was only a couple of thousand dollars but this guy had taken a real liberty. 'I know what you've done and I'm coming to get you,' I told him. This was turning into the Prima affair all over again, but this time I was on his turf.

We set off in my truck and went to find him. When we reached the car park outside his apartment block we could see that his door was open. It looked as if he must have run off, but then I saw something move behind the doorframe. My friend got out of the car and ran over towards the door and I followed him. When I have a temper I can be unpredictable and I don't know what I would have done to him if I'd caught him, but then I stopped dead. I don't know what it was but I felt afraid, as if my life were in danger. I was crossing a line that I hadn't drawn and something told me that I was probably going to pay with my life.

I stood there in the middle of the car park and watched as my friend stormed into the apartment. The door closed behind him.

I just stared. It didn't matter any more. So what if he took my money? He wasn't going to take my life. I got back in the truck and drove away.

I never saw my friend again after that. Maybe they killed him in that apartment the way I think they would have killed me. Who knows? It's easy enough to bury a body where nobody will find it when you live in the middle of the Nevada Desert.

Back in the real world people could see that I had fallen in with a bad crowd and they were talking. There was even a rumour doing the rounds, incorrect as it happens, that I had a gun myself and that I had shot somebody. Mustafa's son worked for the police and he had been listening to stories about what was happening with my gangster buddies, passing on the information to his dad. Mustafa eventually took issue with me about it. He actually came to my home unannounced, walking past the security at the gate and into the house. Even now, I'm not sure how he managed it because the guards were paid to tell me immediately when I had a visitor. 'Who are these punks?' he demanded. Mustafa already knew the answer but he wanted to hear what I thought.

'These are my friends,' I told him.

'These guys are nobody's friends. You brought your family here so that you could fight. We need to get you back to your family, otherwise you're going to end up in jail or dead.'

He was absolutely right. As I looked at him I felt like crying. It was after listening to him that I settled down and started to get my life back under control. Whatever may have happened between us in the past, Mustafa is a dear friend.

Chapter 17

Audrey and Danny

There are some people you can develop a dislike for over a period of time. Danny Williams, for instance, always seemed like a decent guy when I first got to know him and it was only later, after he opened his mouth at the press conference before the Klitschko fight, that he started to get on my nerves.

Then there are other individuals you see for the first time and say to yourself, 'This is a real prat.' For an example of this, look no further than Audley Harrison. I have never liked the guy and I never will. This is somebody who has spent his whole life shouting to anybody who will listen about how great he is and, in the end, he has achieved very little indeed. I cannot think of any other boxer who brought out an autobiography before even turning professional, but that is what the 'A-Force', as he was known, did in 2001. Fair play, he did manage to win the gold medal at the Sydney Olympics, but what has he done since? He should learn to shut his mouth.

Nothing But Trouble

What he doesn't tend to tell people is that he used to work as my sparring partner. While I was world champion and he was still an amateur, he would come to the gym to work with me. I would batter him all over the ring in those sessions.

Audley also used to work as a DJ in London. I walked into a club once where he was playing, not too long before he went to the Olympics, and he started singing my praises over the loudspeakers. Then, after he won the gold medal in Sydney, he started to get a bit full of himself. I bumped into him at Panos's gym in London and said, 'Hello, Audrey.'

'My name is not Audrey,' he said. 'It's Audley, and if you carry on getting it wrong I shall have to ask you to accompany me outside.'

I could see he was annoyed, but at the same time he wasn't serious about the last bit. There was no way he fancied going outside with me. 'I tell you what, Audrey, let's go outside now and if I beat you, I can call you whatever I want.' He went quiet and skulked off.

I don't know what the 'A' in 'A-Force' stands for, even though I can think of a few suitable words, so I will just keep calling him Audrey. When Audrey began his professional career, he started off by fighting a lot of bums. There is no problem with that because all good fighters need to work their way up the professional ranks, gradually improving the quality of their opposition until they are fighting at championship level. Audrey, though, told everybody that he expected to be battling for the British title by his third fight. There were some useful heavyweights around in Britain then, such as Danny Williams, Michael Sprott and Mike Holden, and all of them would have beaten Audrey in his third fight. To me, Audrey's arrogance was sickening and disrespectful, and I wanted to get my hands on him as quickly as possible. I wanted to give him a beating and show him what professional boxing was all about. The problem was that, for all his talk of one day becoming the world champion, he carried on facing limited-quality boxers, first in England and then over in America, for the first four years of his professional career.

Sometimes I think that Audrey had seen me making a noise in the past, telling everybody how good I was, and decided to use that as a template for his own career. The difference is that I was as good as I said I was, and I backed up my words with actions.

The top British heavyweights, including Danny Williams and me, had made it clear that we were willing to fight him. Something Audrey was good at was getting attention, so if Danny or I were to be matched with him, it couldn't fail to be a big event. In my case, a fight looked to be close in 2003. At the end of May Audrey was due to fight another one of his carefully selected victims, Matthew Ellis, at the York Hall in Bethnal Green. The BBC were covering the fight live and they asked me to sit at the ringside so that we could be interviewed together after Audrey had won.

As I watched the fight I was rooting for Audrey, shouting advice to him as he secured a routine victory in the second round. Make no mistake, this wasn't because I was a turning into a fan. Rather, it was in my interests to see Audrey win the fight, or at least I thought it was, because there would be no interest in a fight between us if he was to get beaten.

Nothing But Trouble

Unfortunately, mine wasn't the only name being linked with Audrey's. There had also been talk of his fighting Frank Bruno, even though Frank had been retired for a long time. It would certainly have created public interest, but the way Audrey went about publicising it was all wrong. Bruno was up there in the ring with him as the result was announced. Audrey grabbed the microphone and addressed the crowd: 'I got a couple of rivals in here today who have come to the Audley Harrison show. I just want to ask the public, if it's a question between Frank Bruno and Herbie Hide, who do you say I should fight?'

It was a deliberate attempt to provoke me, and the crowd, who were there to support Audrey, started chanting, 'Bruno! Bruno!' Getting under my skin was one thing, but Audrey had another very clear motive for doing this. The BBC had been pressuring him to take a worthy opponent and by interviewing us together it would make it difficult for him to say, 'No, I want to carry on fighting bums.' In Britain the media are not allowed to conduct interviews inside the ring, so the fighter must come to the ring apron to be interviewed. Audrey didn't want to come to the apron while I was there, so he tried to avoid it by causing some trouble.

While this was going on the BBC were trying to get me to the ring for the interview. The problem was that Audrey's security team were surrounding me and making me feel very uncomfortable. Nobody had touched me, but they were getting very close to me. Then, from out of nowhere, a young woman pushed me. I don't know what she said to me because the noise at ringside made it impossible for me to hear her. She was half-caste and quite pretty.

Audrey and Danny

The crowd were pushing forward and I was starting to feel claustrophobic. Steve Bunce was also at the ringside and he could see that I was starting to lose my cool, so he told me that it was best if I made my way to the exit. That sounded like good advice but I was blocked in, so I had to climb onto one of the press tables in order to get away from the ringside area.

The woman who had pushed me followed me, climbing up onto the table beside me and pushing me twice more, trying to make me lose my balance. I am still not sure what her problem was but she had a very bad attitude. Anyway, I wasn't having that, so I shoved her back and she fell off the table.

After that the place kicked off and, as everyone knows, in England we have the best hooligans in the world. All they need is an excuse to fight and away they go. Crocodile, who had come with me to watch Audrey (after failing to chat up my friend Dawn Noel when he met her at my home, Crocodile had somehow persuaded her to lend us her BMW Z3 convertible for the fight), and I made our way through the crowd to the exit. Chairs were flying all over the place. Then I lost my footing and fell to the floor. Whether I banged my arm on the floor or a chair hit me, I don't know, but whatever happened my watch got broken. It was a diamond-encrusted Rolex, the same as one worn by Tupac Shakur, which I had bought for £85,000. I was gutted about that, not least because I hadn't been able to get it insured for use outside my home. I still have it, or what's left of it, at home in a drawer.

Audrey waited until I was virtually outside the arena before he took the microphone again. 'Oi, security,' he shouted for the television cameras. 'Please, get Herbie Hide out of here.' He said it as if the riot had been my fault. In reality he was trying to score a few cheap points by making himself look as though he were taking charge of the situation. To make matters even worse he apologised to the rabble for me being there in the first place.

The police and the British Boxing Board of Control investigated and, in the end, the Board fined me £500, which wasn't really fair because the riot wasn't of my making. Audrey was fined £1,000. It served him right for causing so much trouble.

A fight between Audrey and Bruno never had any chance of materialising. Bruno, who had been out of the ring for seven years by this point, hadn't fought since Mike Tyson beat him in 1996. I think that even Audrey would have beaten him now. Furthermore, he was also 41 years old and messed around with cocaine as his private life spun out of control. Not long after he'd attended the fight at York Hall, matters came to a head when he was sectioned under the Mental Health Act. A return to boxing was out of the question as he focused on the more serious issue of battling his demons within.

The people in the media aren't blind and they could see that Audrey would do anything to avoid facing any of the more dangerous British fighters out there. The press were getting on his back about it and, after the incident in York Hall, he decided to try his luck in America instead. He based himself in Las Vegas, not far from where I was living at the time.

Audrey obviously thought that insulting and ridiculing me in public was part and parcel of promoting a fight, or at least gaining public attention. As a marketing exercise it worked, but that didn't mean I was about to forgive him, particularly as he had no intention of risking his sorry arse against me in the first place. I made this quite clear to him the next time we spoke. He was at the house of a friend of mine, a guy called Kenny Crumb, who is well known in and around Las Vegas, when I phoned. If I had known that Audrey was going to be there, I wouldn't have bothered, but once Kenny had me on the line he thought I would be happy to talk to another British heavyweight and passed the phone over. Audrey was all sweetness and light, as if nothing had ever happened. 'Listen,' I said. 'After all those things you've been saying about me in the papers and on TV, don't think you are my friend.'

'That was just business,' he said. 'We're cool.'

'Audrey, do yourself a favour. Stay out of my way because you're not safe anywhere near me.'

I think he must have understood because, a few weeks later while I was training at the Top Rank gym, a guy called Del called over to me. 'Hey, Herbie,' he shouted across the gym. 'Your friend Audley in on the way.'

'To this gym? Did you tell him I'm here?'

'No. He's only five minutes away. You can tell him yourself when he gets here.'

'Call him back,' I said. 'Tell him I'm here. I bet you my car that the fucker won't show his face.'

Sure enough, he never came. They are probably still waiting for him there now.

Eventually, Audrey saw that he had to take on some of the tougher guys in the division if he was going to make anything of his career, and that was when he started to lose. He faced Danny Williams in London in 2005 and lost on a split decision. Then he went in with another false alarm, Dominick Guinn, in California in early 2006 and lost again, this time unanimously on the scorecards. He beat Danny in a rematch, but then he was knocked out by Michael Sprott in the third round when they met at Wembley Arena in 2007. Overall, he blew more cold than hot when he stepped up against a better class of opponent.

I am sure that Warren would have loved to have put him in with Samuel Peter, the WBC heavyweight champion, when he was rumoured to be coming to London in July 2008. Audrey wouldn't have wanted it though. The funny thing is, if Audrey took a chance, I think he could beat Peter. I remember watching Tye Fields, a huge American heavyweight, smash Peter all over the gym in sparring. Audrey doesn't have much in the way of talent, but I don't think Peter is that good either. If I was in Audrey's shoes, and somebody offered me the opportunity, it's a fight I would take.

Audrey is one of the fights that got away, but one of the biggest regrets of my boxing career is that I never fought Danny Williams in a boxing match. Everybody knows that I had beaten him up in sparring for years, but that's not really the same. What I really wanted was the opportunity to unload on him in a proper boxing match so that I could show the world that I was the best heavyweight in Britain.

We did get close to fighting each other in 2004, but events overtook us and the fight never took place. The European Union heavyweight title, a poor man's version of the European Boxing Union title, was vacant and they asked Danny to face me for it. Danny was still with Warren at the time, and I was with Mickey, so it was never going to be easy to promote. It went to purse bids and, to everyone's surprise, Jess Harding won the rights to stage it. I thought that Warren would have won the bid. He knew what it was worth and what kind of attention it would generate in Britain. Whatever he had paid for it, he would have been able to make up several times through ticket sales and television rights.

Many experts were calling this a pick-'em fight, one where either boxer could win if things went his way, and he may have felt the same. They may have been right, even if I am sure I would have beaten Danny easily, but Warren knew that Danny blew hot and cold and that if he wasn't on form against me, he would have stood no chance. Danny has had some good victories and on his night he is a very capable boxer, but you must also consider his performances against Sinan Samil Sam and in the last fight with Audrey.

Mickey was disappointed to miss out on it. The fight was perfect for London and he would have liked to have staged it at the Royal Albert Hall or Wembley Arena. Wherever it had taken place, there would have been no problem in selling tickets. Britain has been starved of quality heavyweight boxing for a long time now, so this would have drawn a lot of people. You have only to look at the attendances for the fights between Danny and Audrey or Audrey and Michael Sprott recently to know how popular a fight like this would have been.

Jess says that he would have hired Norwich Sports Village for the fight so that I could fight in front of my home crowd, but I don't think this would have really made sense. You could have filled that place if I was fighting a much less meaningful fight, but this one had the potential to fill a bigger hall in the capital. It had 'London' written all over it. It wouldn't have stopped me fighting though, because, wherever the fight took place, I just wanted to get my hands on Danny.

For Jess this would have been a stepping stone back into television. Audrey and Robin had also moved on and his contract with the BBC had run its course. He had nothing more to offer until this fell into his lap. Promoters know that television revenue is the be-all and end-all in boxing and they are often willing to take chances like this. There are guys out there who are willing to risk a top prospect's career against an established fighter if it means getting a foot in the door with one of the television companies. That's the business side of boxing, and Jess understood it.

Another fight was planned before I could face Danny, against Mindaugas Kulikauskas from Lithuania in March 2003, and it went disastrously wrong. I didn't even know that he was a southpaw before we fought and, even though my training had been going very well, both in Las Vegas and back in England, I hadn't been sparring with any southpaws.

For the first two rounds I struggled and then, in the third, there was a bad clash of heads and I was cut above my left eye. Even though I wanted to continue there was no way I could – the cut was just too deep. I argued with the doctor and the referee but Mickey just said, 'Let him stop it. There's nothing you can do. It's an accident.'

I felt devastated and I needed a few days to pick myself up afterwards. It's one thing to lose when somebody knocks you out, or fights a better fight, but to lose like this was cruel.

While the injury I suffered against Kulikauskas delayed the fight with Danny Williams, another episode of legal trouble put a stop to it altogether. The police in Norwich knew that I would carry on driving, even though the courts had disqualified me. During the day I would stay at home and keep myself to myself, but in the evenings I liked to go out and visit friends. Living where I did in Bawburgh, about seven miles from the city centre, getting around without a vehicle was always going to be tricky.

For a couple of months I did well to avoid the police. Family and friends would watch out for me and tell me when suspicious-looking cars were parked nearby because I never could be too sure when an unmarked police car would be lying in wait.

Eventually, though, the police in Norwich being what they are, I was bound to be brought to book. On 15 May 2003, a couple of weeks before all the trouble with Audrey, they caught me. I was using a Fiat Punto belonging to somebody who had been working at my house – I was known for driving flash motors so I never thought they would recognise me in a car like that – when they spotted me from a lay-by. That was it. They booked me for driving while disqualified.

There were several reasons for my being disqualified in the first place. Since I started making money, and buying cars, I have been stopped a million times. The police, when they stop you, usually demand that you produce your papers. If you don't have them with you, you are requested to present them at the nearest police station within the near future. As I have already mentioned, I have owned several cars, many of which all at the same time, and finding the corresponding insurance documents, or MOT certificates, was sometimes difficult. It could get confusing because I was stopped so often and I couldn't always remember which car I had been driving at that particular time, or where I had been stopped.

Another problem was the fact that, before Helen and I lived together, I would be living on my own and I found it difficult to organise my paperwork. This meant that I was being done for failing to produce my documents from time to time and over the years the points have increased on my licence.

I should also mention that, even though I consider myself to be an excellent driver, I had a number of high-performance vehicles, so it was inevitable that I would be caught speeding from time to time. Again, this also contributed to my points total. Everybody knows what happens when you collect too many points – they disqualify you.

Funnily enough, the police never bothered stopping me when I first started driving. I would have been 17 when I bought a battered old Ford Capri for £150, and I didn't even have a driving licence then. Carmichael Kerr from the Lads' Club would sit in the passenger seat beside me to make sure that I didn't drive too close to the kerb and we would cruise round the city in first gear because I hadn't got the hang of the clutch. It was only when Barry organised a sponsored car for me after I had joined Matchroom that I began taking driving lessons.

The case of driving while disqualified went to court in early 2004, but was rescheduled a couple of times because I was not able to attend. I was back in Las Vegas by this time so my solicitor, Ian Fisher, represented me. They convicted me in my absence and sentenced me to community service. It would be another four years before I would set foot in England again.

Chapter 18

Nigeria

For as long as I can remember, people have asked me if I am British or Nigerian. It seems to matter more to others than it does to me. The honest answer is that I am a man of the world. I go wherever my job calls me, and I have both British and Nigerian passports to get me there. I don't think you could label me as a typical Englishman or a typical Nigerian. Yes, I was born in Africa, but I was educated in England. I enjoy eating in African restaurants, but the mother of my three children is a white girl from Norfolk. My friends come from Africa, from England and from everywhere else on the planet. All in all, I think my character has been moulded by both cultures.

Being British is helpful when you're selling a fight because the man in the street, a British street at any rate, can identify with a fighter from the United Kingdom more than he can with a boxer from Africa – even if both men are one and the same. It's a fact that your name will get you only so far, and nationality is an important factor in marketing the product. However, my African roots are also very important to me. The culture of my people is one I still feel I belong to, even after all these years away. Whenever I get the chance, I go back to Nigeria, where members of my extended family still live and where I now have property to my name.

Nigeria is one of the richest countries in Africa with its oil reserves and agricultural output. It also has a long and complicated history. The troubles are sometimes documented in the press today, with tales of kidnap and corruption tainting its image, but these are relatively recent trends. As I was born, in 1971, Nigeria was in the aftermath of its civil war, also known as the Biafran War, which took place between 1967 and 1970.

A problem in many African nations – and Nigeria is a prime example – is that they have been created by the Europeans who colonised them. Previously, they had been areas made up of several kingdoms, all with their own customs and beliefs. The three main ethnic groups in Nigeria were the Hausa people, a mainly Muslim group from the north of the country, the Yoruba people in the southwest, who were made up of both Muslims and Christians, and my people, the Igbos, who were mainly Christian and lived in the southeast. Once British colonial rule ended in 1960 these groups had to work together to rule the country. At first, parties from the Igbo and Hausa people ruled Nigeria, but in 1965 a fraudulent election saw an alliance of Yoruba and Hausa people assume power.

A coup by Igbo soldiers in 1966 led to military rule, before a countercoup by the Hausa people resulted in another change in power. After this, large numbers of Igbo people who were living in the Muslim north were massacred.

The Nigerian economy in the 1960s had been based on agriculture in the south and mineral deposits in the north but, when oil reserves were discovered in the Niger Delta, the southeast of the country suddenly became a very lucrative territory. The Igbo people became concerned that the Hausa government would strip the area and distribute the wealth in the north. This would have been the last straw after the fraudulent elections and the massacres, and so the southeast broke away in 1967 to form a new nation, the Republic of Biafra.

The Nigerian government refused to accept Biafra's independence and in July 1967 the civil war commenced, with the Nigerian troops attacking Biafra from two sides. The Biafran forces gave a good account of themselves, gaining territory to the west and causing thousands of Nigerian casualties, but once the Nigerian forces reorganised themselves the Biafran troops were forced back into the Igbo heartlands. Once this happened the Nigerians surrounded them and blockaded the routes into Biafra. The people of Biafra were left to starve. The Biafrans surrendered in January 1970 after the fall of Uli, Amichi and my city, Owerri. Millions of my people died as a result of the war. Our hospitals and schools had been destroyed, our homes flattened.

This is the Nigeria I was born into a year and a half later. We lived in the oil-rich territory, but the revenue was being stolen from my people, as my forefathers had feared would be the case before the war. The Nigerian government had waited until the Biafrans were surrounded, unable to leave their homelands, and then changed the currency. After the war our cash reserves were no longer valid and we were forced to exchange it for the new form of money at a ridiculously low rate. We were second-class citizens in our own country.

It's part of Nigerian history and something many of my people are still bitter about, but it's not something I dwell on. As long as I have been alive, Nigeria has been united and I am happy with it that way. As a child you don't know about the political climate and it's hard to compare yourself with people from other parts of the country. All you know in your infant years is the village you have grown up in.

What other Igbo people make of the political scene is for them to decide. What I do know is that my people proved themselves to be extremely resilient and resourceful in the years following the war. Many felt compelled to flee the country and start afresh in other countries, often as refugees. If you take a look at all of the Africans who have established themselves financially in the rest of the world, 80 per cent of them will be from the Igbo areas.

The Igbos are a proud people and their values are steeped in tradition. They are also brilliant businessmen. It has always been the way of our people to build houses and provide employment for the local people. Even after many of the Igbo people were lost in the war, and the currency became all but worthless, the Igbos still wanted to build and provide a foundation for themselves. For those Igbos living outside Nigeria, it is important to come back to the homeland and build two houses. The first is erected in the village where that person was born, the second in one of the large cities. This isn't just for the rich: it is something all men wish to do as part of their cultural heritage. Otherwise, they would one day die of shame.

Without financial assistance from the Nigerian government, the Igbo people have regrouped and built property all over the country. If you look at any major city in Nigeria, at least 75 per cent of the buildings will belong to Igbo landlords. Just visit a place such as Ochicha Ngugo, a communal town near to Owerri, where the Igbo people have built scores of five-to-ten-storey buildings. In an area renowned for oil production, the residents have little to do with the petroleum industry, instead relying on their own enterprise.

Another important feature of the Igbo people is that they do not rely on leaders. Wherever else you look in Africa – and in Nigeria alone there are more than 350 ethnic groups – everybody has a king of some sort. Not so the Igbos. Our people are far too independently minded for that. Every person is capable of making his or her own way to the top.

Looking back at my early childhood, I think we must have been poor. My bed was made of wood, with no mattress, and I would walk around with bare feet most of the time. I did have shoes but they would be used only for special occasions, such as Christmas and weddings. One time I went to put them on and there was something furry inside. I shook the shoe and a mouse fell onto the floor. It just goes to show how rarely I would wear them – even when I went to Glebe House School, my teacher Mr Brearley had to convince me that it was better to run around the athletics track in trainers. Ever since finding that mouse I have always checked inside my shoes before putting them on.

Owerri, situated at the heart of the Igbo territory, is the administrative centre of the Imo state and was at one time the capital of Biafra. The name means open place. We had a small house there where I lived with my mother, my grandmother and my uncles – I never knew my natural father. The round walls were built from red clay, the roof was made of straw and there was only one room. It had been in my family for generations. We would sleep in that room, cook outside and wash at the nearby stream.

As a child, living in a hot country with very little in the way of clothes, you are constantly being bitten by insects and other creatures. Maybe this was more so in my case, as I was always so boisterous, running around all the time without a care. I would have been about six when I was bitten by a snake. The scar is still there on my right shin, hard and shiny and the size of a penny.

I don't like snakes at all. I remember a carpet viper getting into our hut one night while I was trying to sleep. I could hear the noise as it was hunting a lizard in the straw roof above my bed. There were always lizards near the house and the snakes would feed on them. When my grandmother heard what was happening she called the old man from the next house and he took me outside. He brought a stick and a huge knife with him, and poked at the roof with the stick to move the lizard. Once it reached the doorway the viper followed it and poked its head out of the straw. As quick as a flash the old man cut off its head with the knife.

Years later, when I was living in Las Vegas and

training in the Red Rock Canyon, I would kill snakes myself if I saw them, whacking them with a stick. They are horrible creatures.

Parasites were also a problem where I lived. Like many children in the area, I had worms living in my legs. You wouldn't always know that they were there, but when they reached a certain size you could see them below the skin. The Nigerians would deal with them by rubbing oil on the affected area, which would heat up the skin and dry out the worms.

There was also a time when I had something living on my dick. Before you start asking how it got there, I was a young child of seven and I didn't yet know what sex was. These infections would just happen. There is still a hole there from the wound it left.

You can imagine what the local school would have been like. When I bothered going, which was not very often, we would sit on benches in another mud hut. There was an open doorway and a window with no glass in it. We would use a slate and chalk to copy down our teacher's words. It was just how the African schools look on television.

Building in a country like Nigeria isn't always easy. As with all Igbo men, it's something I had wanted to do ever since I was young and, after Alan died, I decided to take the plunge. Owerri is made up of several villages and in those villages everybody is related in one way or another. The land there is owned by the various families and, if you belong to one of those families and you want to build, they will give you the land. I was given a plot of land on which to build in the area where my family lived, and began work on a house there.

Nothing But Trouble

Problems arose when some of the local people become jealous. I had been away from Nigeria for a while since starting work on the house and when I went back there we could see that somebody had been practising witchcraft on the property. It's something that many people believe in, not just in Nigeria, but all over Africa, and there are many types of magic and spells that can be used to curse a person. In this case they had sacrificed a chicken, among other things, leaving blood and feathers on a plate in the middle of the floor. Many people would have sought advice from the elders and perhaps called a witch doctor to cleanse the place of evil. This would have been a long-winded process and I didn't have time, so I cleared up the mess myself and threw it away. My mum is much more superstitious than I am and the whole situation frightened her. She was afraid that the curse would bring harm to our family. In the end we abandoned the house, leaving it unfinished.

In 2004 I started work on a property in the exclusive Asokoro district of Abuja, the Nigerian capital. Virtually all of the Nigerian Cabinet members live in this part of the city, and the presidential palace, called Aso Rock, is also located here. My neighbours in Asokoro are Nigerian statesmen and business leaders and, now that the house is complete, the value is estimated at £1.5 million. It's a long way removed from my family's hut in Owerri.

In November of that year I visited Abuja to see how the house was progressing. I had paid the contractor in advance and expected the job to be nearly finished. When I arrived there the building work was only half completed, so I went to see him and demanded my money back. He contacted the police.

Nigeria

The police came for me and took me at gunpoint to a station in Karu on the outskirts of the city. Abuja is a wealthy, purpose-built city, but at its edges there are shanty towns that house the poorer people. Karu doesn't even have running water or electricity. I tried to bribe my way out of there but the officer in charge refused, telling me that I would have to stay in a cell. It was disgusting in there. There must have been 20 other inmates, all packed into a room half the size of a boxing ring. It was a hot day and inside the cell it was sweltering. It was hard to breathe and the smell was overpowering. Some of the prisoners were trying to sleep, resting their heads on the next man's shoulder because that was all the space they could find.

Being arrested is something I was used to in Norwich but nothing could have prepared me for this place. When I was brought in I had had about £4,000 in my pocket, but the police took that from me. My cellmates wanted to see if I would give them some money too, but by this point I didn't have any left. They left me alone after that.

In the centre of the room was a latrine. It was nothing more than a hole in the floor covered by a metal plate. I needed to pee but I didn't fancy using this facility. Instead, I asked the inmate next to me what I would need to do if I wanted to poo. He told me that I would have to use the hole. At first I thought he was joking with me but then, literally two seconds later, another prisoner dropped his trousers and started crapping. There was no paper but I guess that somebody who uses a toilet like that probably isn't too fussy about his personal hygiene. They kept me there for about two hours, until my

237

Nothing But Trouble

business partners turned up. It was a very interesting experience, but not one I would like to repeat.

In the end I was forced to bring in a new builder to complete the project at my own expense. Such are the risks of undertaking work in Nigeria.

Chapter 19

Hamburg and Beyond

T he money in America wasn't enough for me. It's OK
if you are being featured on HBO, or even on
Showtime, where they have the resources to pay the top
boxers very well, but I wasn't on their books so I decided
to look elsewhere to earn a living. Europe was the only
place where I thought I would be able to get paid a
reasonable rate. Moving back to the UK would have been
an option, but I wasn't sure where I stood legally with the
driving conviction and community service still hanging
over me like a black cloud. The other big country for
boxing in Europe was Germany, where the sport has
experienced a huge boom in recent years. That's why, in
March 2007, I decided to accept the promoter Ahmet
Oener's offer and join his stable in Hamburg.

Ahmet used to be a fighter himself. He was a useful
boxer who won a couple of domestic belts in Germany in
the late 1990s. He ended his career inside the ring in 2002
having won 15 and drawn 2 of his 23 fights and

concentrated then on the management side of boxing. At first he advised the Turkish heavyweight Sinan Samil Sam.

In 2006 he founded Arena Box-Promotion in Hamburg, signing contracts with established boxers such as Sinan and Juan Carlos Gomez, the Cuban heavyweight who used to be the WBC cruiserweight champion, as well as several up-and-coming fighters.

I liked what I saw and Ahmet promised that I would be boxing regularly, under the tutelage of my new trainer, Bulent Baser. The gym was good and I wanted to get my head down and begin training. The change in the weight regulations meant that the cruiserweight limit had been lifted to 200lb (91kg), which, for somebody like me, who had always been small at heavyweight, was ideal. The heavyweights were getting bigger and bigger but at cruiserweight I had a real chance to succeed.

Although Ahmet grew up in Duisburg in one of the poorest areas of the city, he was actually born in Istanbul. In Germany there are several large Turkish communities, particularly in the larger cities, and Ahmet is very close to his Turkish roots. Indeed, many of the boxers at the gym come from Turkey and when Ahmet has time he will often spend time with them, eating Turkish food and speaking the Turkish language.

But there are several other nationalities at the gym and it has a very cosmopolitan feel to it with boxers from Germany, Africa, Cuba and Russia. This is the way in which boxing has become so successful in Germany in the recent past: fighters with potential are brought in from poorer countries and groomed alongside the native boxers, so there is a far larger pool of talent available to the promoters.

Hamburg and Beyond

Several boxers have joined the stable since my arrival, the highest-profile of them being Odlanier Solís, Yuriolkis Gamboa and Yan Barthelemí, the three Cubans who won gold at the Olympic Games in Athens. They had to defect from Cuba just to be able to join the professional ranks and now all three of them are well on their way to becoming outstanding fighters.

Ahmet wanted me to start fighting very quickly and by the end of my first month I had appeared on one of his shows in Hamburg against an Estonian called Valery Semishkur, beating him in the first round before telling the assembled media, 'Call the police, because the bad boy is back.'

That was the first of five fights that year. They were all fairly straightforward wins against unheralded opposition from Eastern Europe – although when I fought Mikhail Nasyrov, an unbeaten Russian, for the WBC International title in Halle two days before Christmas, he did ask me one or two questions. I had him down three times in the second round and I thought that would have been the end of it, but he came back at me with a second wind three rounds later. In the sixth, I took charge again, smashing him with two right hands and then a left uppercut, forcing the referee to wave it off.

It was only a small hall and the timing of the event may have put a lot of people off, but I had a lot of support from my African friends from Hamburg, and having Ian Allcock helping in my corner was a real plus.

I returned to Halle to make the first defence of my title. The Christmas show was meant to be a homecoming for my stablemate Steffen Kretschmann, but he had to pull out on that occasion due to injury.

Nothing But Trouble

Ahmet wanted to go back there to give Steffen another chance to appear before his home supporters, and I was billed as the headline act. My opponent was Rudiger May, a man who had challenged Johnny Nelson for the WBO title in 2004. He was a spoiler, tall and rangy, and not very nice to look at at all. Rudiger had won more than 40 fights but most of them had been by decision. He had also lost a few, including the one against Johnny, who stopped him in the seventh.

My plan was to get him early. I had been suffering with illness during training and I wasn't as fit as I would have liked to be, so I didn't want to waste energy by chasing him all night. He was quick on his feet but, as is often the case with nimble boxers, he didn't have much power in his fists. His quick footwork didn't make any difference because I followed him all over the ring and landed some hurtful shots. He was getting through with one or two of his own punches too, but they weren't heavy enough to bother me. At the end of the first round I caught him with an overhand right and then put him down by following up with a left hook. When he was down, the adrenalin got the better of me and I hit him once more for good measure. Ahmet was up in my corner at the break, telling me that I was crazy and that I needed to calm down. When Rudiger came out for the second round he was holding on for dear life. He knew that I would put him away sooner or later, and once I had him in the corner I battered him to the floor.

In May 2008 we travelled to Spain for an Arena promotion in the city of Bilbao. I was to fight against a US-based boxer from Benin called Ehinomen Ehikhamenor. On paper he looked a lot easier than he turned out to be. He had won 12 of his 14 fights and stopped 7 of his victims, but there weren't any notable names on his record. There were people who thought that I would be able to beat him in the first or second round, but Ehikhamenor achieved something that nobody else had ever managed: he lasted 12 rounds with me.

Because I have knocked out most of the fighters I have beaten, people tend to believe that I am a banger, somebody who goes looking to land the big shots. This isn't actually the case. I am more of a boxer who likes people to come forward so that I can catch them with my heavy punches while they are moving towards me. I do have power in both hands, but my style is based more on my movement and reflexes rather than my punching ability.

With Ehikhamenor I had a frustrating night. He moved away from me for the whole fight, meaning that I was forced to chase him. Defensively, he was very good and I found it very difficult to hit him. What you cannot hit you can't stop, and so it was that, for only the second time in my career, we went to the scorecards.

Thankfully, I had been training hard and I was fit enough not to have any conditional problems later in the fight. I always knew that the judges would decide in my favour, but it was still a disappointment for me not to have stopped him. I will say this for Ehikhamenor though: he is a lot better than his record suggests, and I think he may be seen in one or two more meaningful cruiserweight fights in the next couple of years.

What was interesting was that Danny Williams was also fighting on the bill in Bilbao. He had tried to clear the air with me before, asking Ian Allcock to pass on his best wishes when he worked in my corner for the Mikhail Nasyrov fight. I didn't take much notice at the time because I knew that I would win that fight, with or without Danny's encouragement.

We were in separate hotels in Bilbao and I hoped that we would be able to stay out of each other's way. However, Danny made a point of coming over to me at the weigh-in to apologise for his comments at the Klitschko press conference. I told him to stay out of my way at first, but on reflection it was a brave thing he did. I could see how nervous he was about talking to me and he still found it within himself to approach me. That took some guts on his part and after that there was very little I could do but accept the apology. I just said to myself, 'I'm thirty-six years old. Do I really need this any more?' And with that we were finally able to put the past behind us.

Seeing Danny shaking like that gave me a feeling of power. Being in Germany for over a year, where very few people even recognise me, I had forgotten that there are many people who find me intimidating. Bülent Baser, my trainer since I joined Arena, was amazed. He had no idea that such a big guy could be so frightened of me.

My hectic schedule continued and there were only a couple of weeks to relax before we travelled to Turkey to prepare for my next opponent, Nuri Seferi. The card had originally been planned for Istanbul but Ahmet moved the show to Ankara because it was Sinan's home city, and Sinan was topping the bill.

I stayed in Ankara from early June until after the fight, although I would have preferred to train in Hamburg.

Hamburg and Beyond

One of the problems for me was the sparring – there wasn't any, at least not at first. I could have sparred but I had a choice of either Sinan or Henry Akinwande, who by now had joined me at Arena and was getting ready for his first fight. As far as I was concerned there was very little point in sparring with either of them. Seferi was a 5ft 11in (1.8m) cruiserweight while Sinan and Henry were both huge heavyweights. It wasn't the kind of practice I needed, but eventually I did manage to spar a few rounds against some proper cruiserweights.

Seferi was also a former sparring partner of mine, from the time I first arrived in Germany, and I had never had any difficulty with him in those sessions. That's why I wasn't really worried about facing him. Unlike Ehikhamenor, Seferi was the kind of fighter who would come forward and let me fight my kind of fight.

It should have been so easy, but it wasn't. Seferi floored me with a left hook after 15 seconds and then had me in trouble again in the second. I had to pull myself together and box for the remaining rounds to get out with the decision. Seferi was much more difficult than he should have been, but much of that was down to me. This was the second time I had been 12 rounds in a matter of weeks and I was exhausted. The snap was missing from my punches. My usual spark and nastiness had deserted me and I never looked as if I would knock him out.

There may be various reasons for my poor display in Ankara, but I think overtraining was one of the fundamental ones. In the 16 months since I had arrived in Hamburg, I had fought 8 times, all over Europe. I had been in the gym virtually every day, trying to build myself up to championship level, and it had been too much.

Nothing But Trouble

The way I was training, especially during those weeks I spent in Turkey, didn't help me much either. Even on the plane as we were travelling over, there was an argument between Sinan and Bulent about how he was training me. Sinan thought I was losing weight too quickly, and that by doing so it would sap my strength. I cannot argue with that, especially as the last 8 ¾lb came off the day before the fight. Then there was the running. We would be out on the streets at 10 o'clock in the morning, just as it was beginning to get hot. As a black man, with my dark skin absorbing the heat, I suffered more than most. Again, what should have been building up my stamina was probably doing just the opposite.

I had to remember that I was 36 and I couldn't operate like this any longer. Conserving my energy was important at this stage of my career. Things were beginning to come to a head and I needed to take a break before I burnt myself out.

Even though I wasn't satisfied with the way things were being done in Turkey – and I have to admit that I was glad to get back to Hamburg the day after the fight – it was still an interesting trip and I was pleased to get to know some of the local people there. Many of the Turkish people are football mad and while I was there much of their attention was focused on the Turkish team, who were playing in the European Championships in Austria and Switzerland. As I have already said, I am not much of a football fan but I wanted the Turks to do well and was bitterly disappointed when they lost to Germany in the semi-final.

There are a lot of Turkish people in Germany, many more than in the United Kingdom, and at first I didn't like them very much. Individually they seemed OK, but in groups I thought they could be quite arrogant. Once I had visited Turkey for the first time my opinion changed. In their homeland they are the most loving, generous people. The boxing fans there treated me like a hero, even though they probably didn't really know who I was. It was then that I understood why a number of the Germany-based Turks, although certainly not all of them, were so unfriendly in Germany.

The Turks are a proud and hard-working people and, after years of helping to build up the German economy for very little pay, they want to be treated as equals in German society. It reminded me of a song by Bob Marley called 'Crazy Baldheads', in which he sings, 'I and I build a cabin / I and I plant the corn / Didn't my people before me / Slave for this country? / Now you look me with a scorn, / Then you eat up all my corn.' The younger generation of Turks want to be respected in the way the African-Americans did after slavery was abolished in the US.

Arriving back in Germany made me realise what a nice life I had there. Living in a hotel for weeks on end is never much fun, and I was happy to be able to go back to my small flat. I had made lots of friends in Hamburg, particularly in the African community there, and it was good to go out and meet people, have a drink and eat African food.

Sometimes I look at my kids and feel very blessed. It's not easy for them, or for Helen, when I am away for such long periods of time. The recent years have been difficult for everybody, with the move to America and back, but they have come through it well. When they have been over to Hamburg to visit me, all of us crammed into my little flat in Niendorf, it has been wonderful to have the family together again.

Henry has a sensible head on his shoulders. He's a good boy and I'm very proud of him. He's modest too, which isn't always easy for a child of that age with a famous father. Now that he is back at school in Norfolk he plays football and recently the kids were invited to an open day at Norwich City. Leon McKenzie, the footballing son of Clinton McKenzie and the nephew of Duke, was on hand and I asked Henry if he had mentioned that he was my son.

'No,' he said. 'I didn't think of it.'

'What do you mean, you didn't think of it?' I asked him. 'All the Norwich players know who I am. You should have said something.' But that's just Henry being Henry.

When he came over to Hamburg in the spring of 2008 he asked me when I would be coming home. 'All you need to do is be good,' he said. 'It's easy to be good.' He's so right.

Haley is the drama queen of the family. She takes after me in that respect. She's much more temperamental than Henry. She was in tears as we last said goodbye.

The fact is, I was ready to come home. I knew it would be beneficial for my family, and for my boxing career too. My name is still very marketable in the UK and now that I can fight on British promotions I feel much better.

On Wednesday, 20 August 2008, over four years since I had last set foot in Britain, I made my long-awaited return to Norwich. It was a weird feeling after being away from home for so long. Helen was away in America to attend a court case concerning our Las Vegas home but the kids were there with my parents and I was looking forward to seeing them all again.

My solicitor, Simon Nichols, had been working hard to sort out my legal situation and, thankfully, the courts accepted that if I returned, I would be allowed to complete 50 hours of community service. This was a weight off my mind because it meant that I would be able to get on with my day-to-day life in Norwich. I wanted to be a family man again, playing with my kids and taking them to McDonald's, all the things that I hadn't been able to do while I was living in Hamburg.

I had already done community service in the past, shortly after Alan's death, when I'd got into an altercation with the police in Norwich after they had pulled me over in the Bentley. There is normally something useful that talented people can do in this situation and I had hoped then that I would be able to teach kids to box, or help elderly people to keep fit. Instead, they sent me out with a shovel and had me digging holes for 60 hours. This time I hoped to do something more worthwhile that could benefit people in the community. There was no hope of that though. In the first week of September I was sent out to work in the gardens of Norwich, tidying up churchyards and playgrounds.

Hamburg hadn't always been an easy place for me to live but I had made the most of it. I was living in a poxy little flat, I had no car, and at first I didn't know many people there. I trained virtually every day while I was there, and the money I made I sent home to the family. But I was content there with the life that I had built up for myself. I made friends and I had everything I needed. As well as this, I knew that I could return home one day, so I never felt like a lost soul. Norwich was still there and was just waiting for me to return.

My uncles had been living in the house during the time that I was away and the place looked a mess. In future, apart from Helen and the kids, whose home it is, I will let only my parents stay there.

But it was still lovely to be home, getting back to the routine of putting the kids to bed in the evening and going running in the mornings with Neil Featherby. Steve and Jackie were delighted to see me again, provided I remembered to take off my shoes.

Looking back, I think I can be satisfied with what I have accomplished. Yes, perhaps I could have achieved much more and ruled the heavyweight division for a long time, but I could also have done a lot worse. Who would have thought that the shy African boy with the stammer would become a two-time world champion? Consider the British boxing stars of the 1990s, fighters such as Chris Eubank, Frank Bruno, Nigel Benn and Naseem Hamed, and it seems like a lifetime ago. I was every bit as much of a superstar as those men in that era, and I'm still here.

Perhaps I don't have long left as a fighter. Age catches up with all of us and I came to prominence while I was very young. It's only logical that I will need to stop one day soon, when my body won't match my will to win. But that day has not yet arrived. I still believe that I have plenty to offer and that there are more titles for me to win. A world championship at cruiserweight is my ultimate ambition, but becoming the oldest man to win a Lonsdale belt outright would also be a major achievement.

Time moves on and there are now new boxers who have their names up in lights. Ricky Hatton, Britain's biggest boxing star, is nearing the end of his career but he hadn't even made his professional debut when I beat Tony Tucker in 1997. Joe Calzaghe was only a prospect then, and nobody had even heard of David Haye or Amir Khan.

The guys I knew as a young boxer continue their lives away from the sport. Francis Ampofo now runs a chicken farm in Norfolk; Scott Welch has invested in residential homes for the elderly; and Jess Harding manages a business in Essex that supplies pallets.

Against all the odds, I have survived them all. I am still here and still fighting. That's an accomplishment in itself.

Appendix

AMATEUR RING RECORD

1988	2 November	S Potter	RSC	
	9 November	S Drew	RSC	1
	8 December	S Wright	PTS	3
	12 December	M Carr	PTS	3
1989	7 January	M Palmer	KO	1
	13 January	M Carr	KO	1
	4 March	M Brown	PTS	3
		Eastern Counties vs		
		Midland Counties		
		zones finals		
	18 March	N Smith	RSC	1
		ABA quarter final		
	5 April	D Browne	RSC	3
		ABA semi-final		
	18 April	H Akinwande	LPTS	3

PROFESSIONAL RING RECORD

1989	24 October	Lee Williams, York Hall, London, England	KO	2
	5 November	Gary McCrory, Royal Albert Hall, London, England	TKO	1
	19 December	Steve Osborne, York Hall, London, England	TKO	6
1990	27 June	Alex Penarski, Royal Albert Hall, London, England	TKO	3
	5 September	Steve Lewsam, Conference Centre, Brighton, England	TKO	4
	26 September	Jonjo Greene, Bowlers Club, Manchester, England	TKO	1
	17 October	Gus Mendes, York Hall, London, England	KO	2
	18 November	Steve Lewsam, National Exhibition Centre, Birmingham, England	TKO	1
1991	29 January	Lennie Howard, Hudson's Sports Centre, Wisbech, England	TKO	1
	9 April	David Jules, Grosvenor House, London, England	TKO	1
	14 May	John Westgarth, Town Hall, Dudley, England	TKO	4
	3 July	Tucker Richards, International Centre, Brentwood, England	TKO	3

Appendix

15 October	Eddie Gonzales, Legien Center, Hamburg, Germany	KO	2
29 October	Chris Jacobs, Star Leisure Centre, Cardiff, Wales	KO	1
1992 21 January	Conroy Nelson, Sports Village, Norwich, England WBC International heavyweight title	TKO	2
3 March	Percell Davis, Jaap Edenhal, Amsterdam, Netherlands	KO	1
8 September	Jean Chanet, Sports Village, Norwich, England	TKO	8
6 October	Craig Petersen, Arenahal, Antwerp, Belgium WBC International heavyweight title	TKO	7
12 December	James Pritchard, Alexandra Pavilion, London, England	TKO	2
1993 30 January	Juan Antonio Diaz, International Centre, Brentwood, England WBA Pentacontinental heavyweight Title	TKO	3
27 February	Michael Murray, Goresbrook Leisure Centre, Dagenham, England British heavyweight title	TKO	5
5 May	Jerry Halstead, Sports Village, Norwich, England WBB heavyweight title	TKO	4

	Date	Opponent	Result	Round
	18 September	Everett Martin, Granby Halls, Leicester, England	PTS	10
	6 November	Mike Dixon, York Hall, London, England WBC International heavyweight title	TKO	9
	4 December	Jeff Lampkin, Superbowl, Sun City, South Africa WBC International heavyweight title	TKO	2
1994	19 March	Michael Bentt, New Den, London, England WBO heavyweight title	KO	7
1995	11 March	Riddick Bowe, MGM Grand, Las Vegas, United States	KOby	6
		WBO heavyweight title	TKO	6
1996	6 July	Michael Murray, Nynex Arena, Manchester, England		
	9 November	Frankie Swindell, Nynex Arena, Manchester, England	KO	1
1997	28 June	Tony Tucker, Sports Village, Norwich, England WBO heavyweight title	TKO	2
1998	18 April	Damon Reed, Nynex Arena, Manchester, England WBO heavyweight title	TKO	1
		Willi Fischer, Sports Village, Norwich, England WBO heavyweight title	TKO	2

Appendix

1999 26 June   Vitali Klitschko, New   KOby 2
                        London Arena, London,
                        England
                        WBO heavyweight title

2001 14 July   Alexei Osokin, Olympia,   TKO   3
                        Liverpool, England

       22 September   Joseph Chingangu, Telewest TKOby 2
                        Arena, Newcastle, England

2003 16 April   Derek McCafferty, Ice   TKO   7
                        Arena, Nottingham,
                        England

       27 May   Joseph Chingangu,   KO   1
                        Goresbrook Leisure
                        Centre, Dagenham,
                        England

       4 October   Alexander Vasiliev,   TKO   5
                        Alexandra Palace,
                        London, England

2004 12 March   Mindaugas Kulikauskas,   TKOby 3
                        Ice Arena, Nottingham,
                        England

2006 23 September   Mitch Hicks, Convention   TKO   1
                        Center, Fort Smith,
                        United States

2007 24 March   Valery Semishkur,   KO   1
                        Sporthalle Alsterdorf,
                        Hamburg, Germany

       27 April   Pavol Polakovic, Arena   KO   6
                        Gym, Hamburg, Germany

       16 June   Aleh Dubiaha, Atatürk   KO   1
                        Sport Salonu, Ankara,
                        Turkey

21 September	Mircea Telecan, Hansehalle, Luebeck, Germany	TKO	1
23 December	Mikhail Nasyrov, Maritim Hotel, Halle an der Saale, Germany WBC International cruiserweight title	TKO	6
2008 11 March	Rudiger May, Maritim Hotel, Halle an der Saale, Germany WBC International cruiserweight title	TKO	2
30 May	Ehinomen Ehikhamenor, Pabellon Lasesarre, Baracaldo, Spain WBC International cruiserweight title	PTS	12
4 July	Nuri Seferi, Bueyuek Anadolu Hotel, Ankara, Turkey WBC International cruiserweight title	PTS	12
18 November	Lukasz Rusiewicz, Kugelbake-Halle, Cuxhaven, Germany	PTS	6